BEAD WEAVING
E L E G A N C E

by TAKAKO SAKO

TRANSLATED FROM JAPANESE

edited by Jules & Kaethe Kliot

LACIS PUBLICATIONS

Material in this book is from the original Japanese language works by Takako Sako:

GLASS BEADS WORK, ISBN 4-8377-0286-4 ©1986 Takako Sako
GLASS BEAD WORK, ISBN 4-8377-0489-1 ©1989 Takako Sako
published by MACAW

The instructions presented in this book assume some general knowledge of bead weaving. Instructions for loom set up will depend on specific loom used and reference should be made to manufacturer's instructions. Specific instructions offered in this book are a translation from the Japanese as originally offered by the author with minor editing as required for clarity.

Reference should be made to the publication
BEAD WEAVING: ACCESSORIES by Takako Sako
published by LACIS PUBLICATIONS
for basic loom weaving and finishing techniques.

All dimensions are given in metric units, unchanged from the original Japanese language editions. To convert millimeters to inches, multiply by .0394. For example 20mm equals .79 inches.

Specific beads and hardware items shown in this book might not be readily available. Inquiries can be made to publisher for current sources of supplies and alternatives.
Bead references are for #11 seed beads, colors shown on inside of back cover. Code numbers are that of Japanese *Toho Best Beads,* distributed in the US by Mill Hill, PO Box 1060, Janesville, WI 53547-1060.
A wide, 11" weaving loom, illustrated on page 128, specifically designed for two-needle bead weaving is available from this publisher.

English language edition published by
LACIS PUBLICATIONS
3163 Adeline Street
Berkeley, CA 94703

ISBN 1-891656-14-7
Printed in China

Front Cover
Reticule (Money Pouch)
Instructions on page 80

Back Cover
Parasol Brooch
Instructions on page 86

CONTENTS

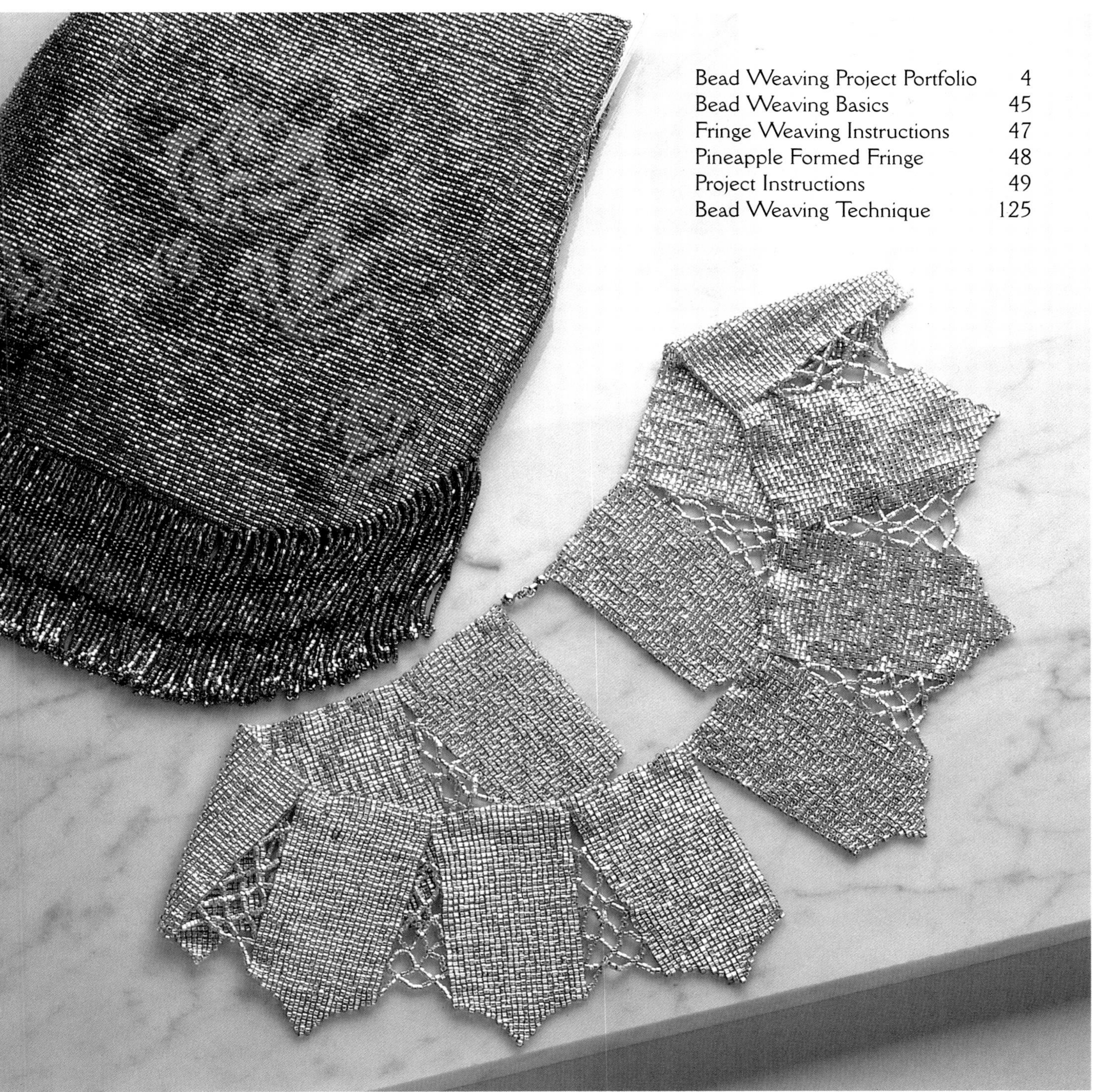

Crystal Collar
Instructions on page 69

A
B

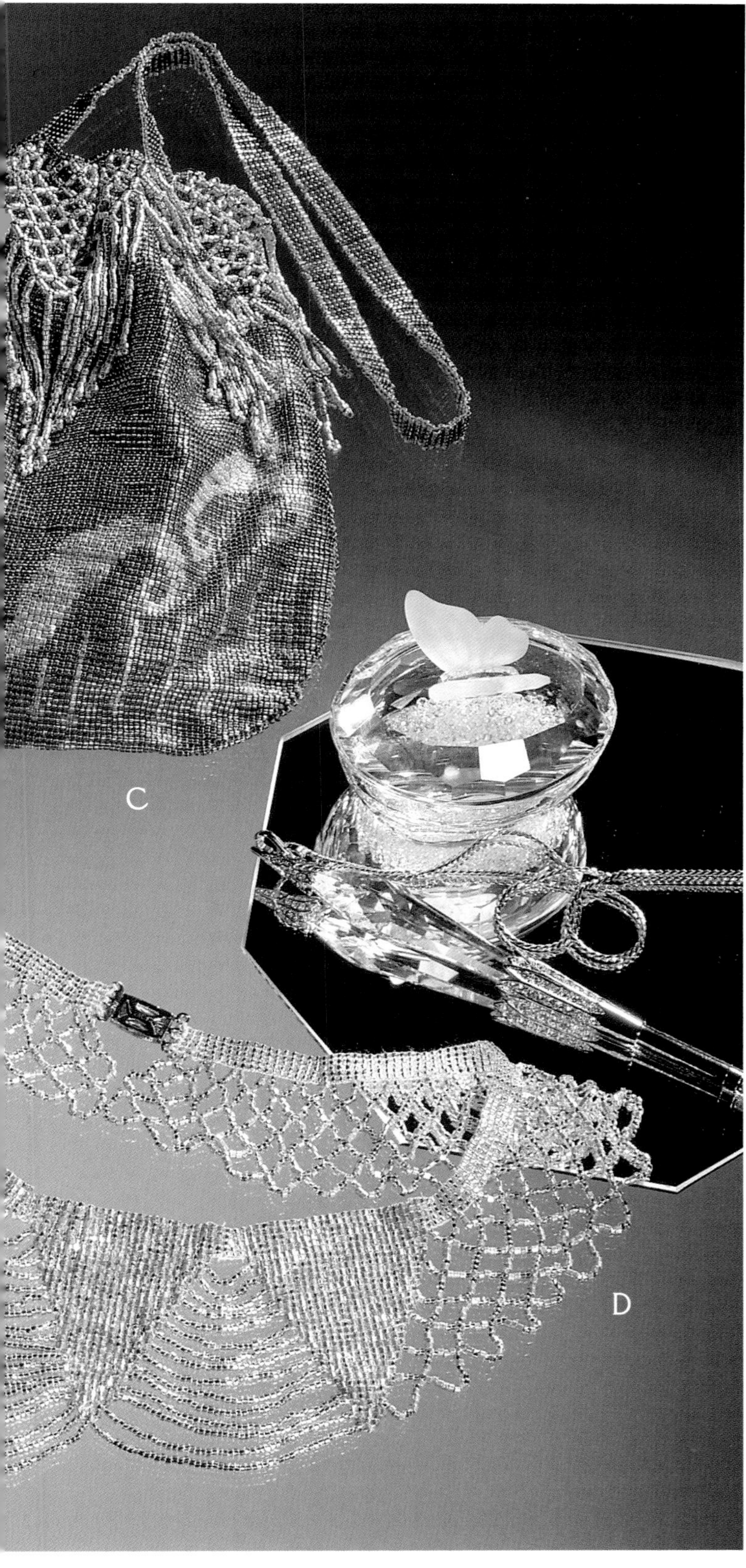

Crystal Afternoon

Draw String Bag (A)
Instructions on page 76

Crystal Pendant (B)
An amulet for scents or pictures. Weave in a triangle, piece two panels together and attach loop fringes to embellish. Increase fringe lengths toward base to emphasize shape. Weave neck band 4 beads wide and attach metal findings.

Graceful Bag (C)
Instructions on page 76

Evening Collar (D)
Instructions on page 68

A Street Corner in London

Winter Corsage (A)
Instructions on page 69

Leaf Necklace (B)
Weave three leaves and join to make a striking collar. Use leaf pattern from Winter Corsage, page 69

Paisley Brooch (C)
Instructions on page 84

"Parisienne" Bag (D)
Instructions on page 78

D
B
C

A
B
C
D
E
F
G
H
I
J

Poems & Fairy Tales

Cattleya (A)
Instructions on page 61

Heart (B)
Instructions on page 63

Tulip (C)
Instructions on page 62

Radish (D)
Instructions on page 78

Christmas Tree (E)
Instructions on page 65

Lily (F)
Instructions on page 62

Flower Girl (G)
22 beads per row. Extend skirt of girl with wavelike fringe producing the effect of a flared skirt. Hanging cord made from 2 twisted strands. Use clear colors for flower bouquet.

Echo (H)
Instructions on page 64

Madam Fumi (I)
Instructions on page 82

Diamond (J)
Instructions on page 50

Flower (K)
Instructions on page 82

Window (L)
Instructions on page 49

Camel (M)
Instructions on page 54

Rainbow (N)
Slightly curve hem. For chain, extend beaded warp threads from panel.

White House (O)
Instructions on page 65

Party (P)
Instructions on page 81

Flower Pinwheel (Q)
Instructions on page 61

Slit (A)
Instructions on page 66

Tulip (B)
A combination of silver and gold beads. The band is woven with three lines as in Braided Band (C).

Braided (C)
Instructions on page 67

Butterfly (D)
Instructions on page 83

Rose (E)
Instructions on page 83

Leaf (F)
Instructions on page 63

Scent Bag (G)
Instructions on page 68

Rhombus (H)
Join diamond pendant and band with beads. Make a hem by folding and stitching 1 cm at top ends of band. Join pendant and band putting strands through the hem several times. Fit metal

Petite Fleur

Necklaces • Bracelet • Pendants • Pouches • Earrings

clasp at the end of bands.

Cylinder (I)
Tie 5 beaded panels, woven in 21 beads x 24 rows, into cylinders. See scent bag, page 67, for instructions.

Clover Pouch (J)
Illustration only

Secret Box (K)
Instructions on page 64

Family Rose (L)
Instructions on page 52

Small Flower (M)
A reproduction of an old bracelet woven in wine and ivory color beads.

Parasol (N)
Instructions on page 86

A
B
C
D
E

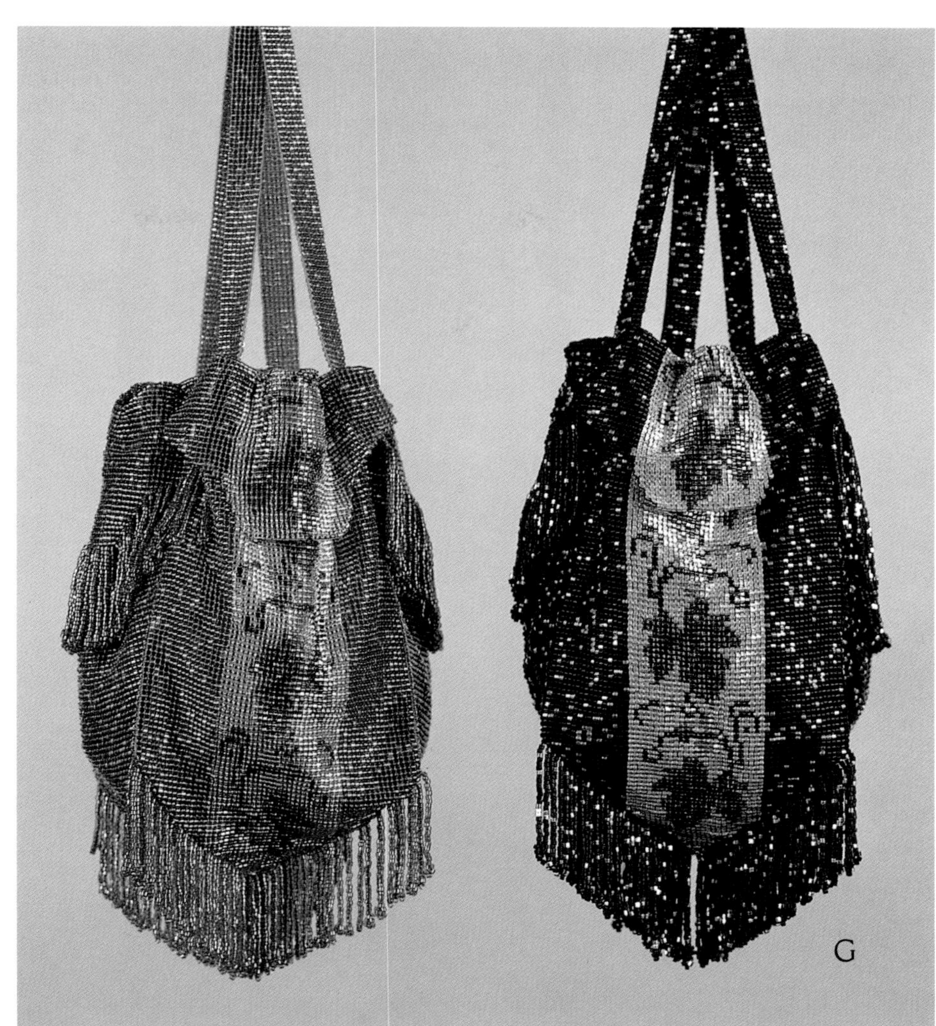

Antique (G)
Instructions on page 87

Roses in May (A)
Instructions on page 72

Rose Arch (B)
Instructions on page 73

Promenade (C)
Instructions on page 75

Rose Pouch (D)
Rimmed with gold beads on the outside framing roses in tones of light pink and white and small red flowers.

Spring Breeze (E)
Instructions on page 71

Family Crest (F)
Instructions on page 85

The Rose

Eyeglass Cases • Pouches • Necktie

A
B

Glittering Ball

Party Bags

Spring in Paris (A)
Illustration only

Memory (B)
Inspired by a goblin spectacle case I was presented with in Europe as a souvenir. Bags with beads, having various kinds of flowers, are woven in patterns of bright color.

Liz (C)
Illustration only

Poem in Miyabi
(Graceful Poem)

Small Bags • Belt • Sashes

Wild Rose (A)
Instructions on page 87

Twill Pattern (B)
Instructions on page 57

Rose (C)
Instructions on page 56

Melody (D)
Instructions on page 70

Ripples (E)
Instructions on page 70

Vertical Frame (F)
Instructions on page 70

B
C
D
E
F

Tsuji-Ga-Hana

Party Bag

This traditional Japanese pattern is typically dyed with uncolored spots. When I first saw this design I was impressed with its tenderness, depth, gentle line and fine hue, and I captured this impression in this bead work. It would be very interesting to weave designs from traditional kimonos for bags.

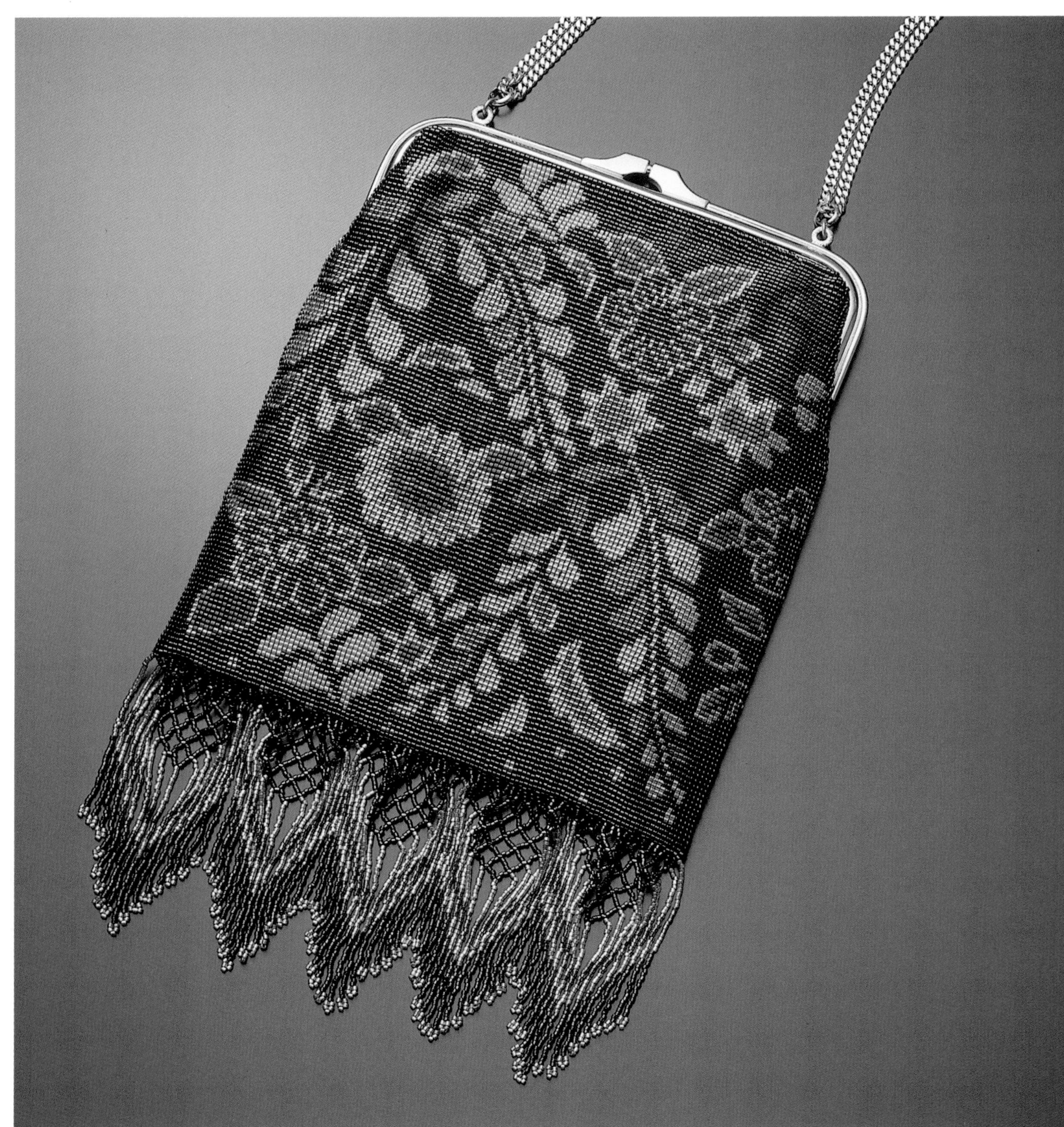

Spring Rhythm

Inspiration from antiques. A small souvenir
from the heart.
Woven into a small choker, fashion
becomes part of Spring's aroma.

Cherry Choker (A)
Instructions on page 93

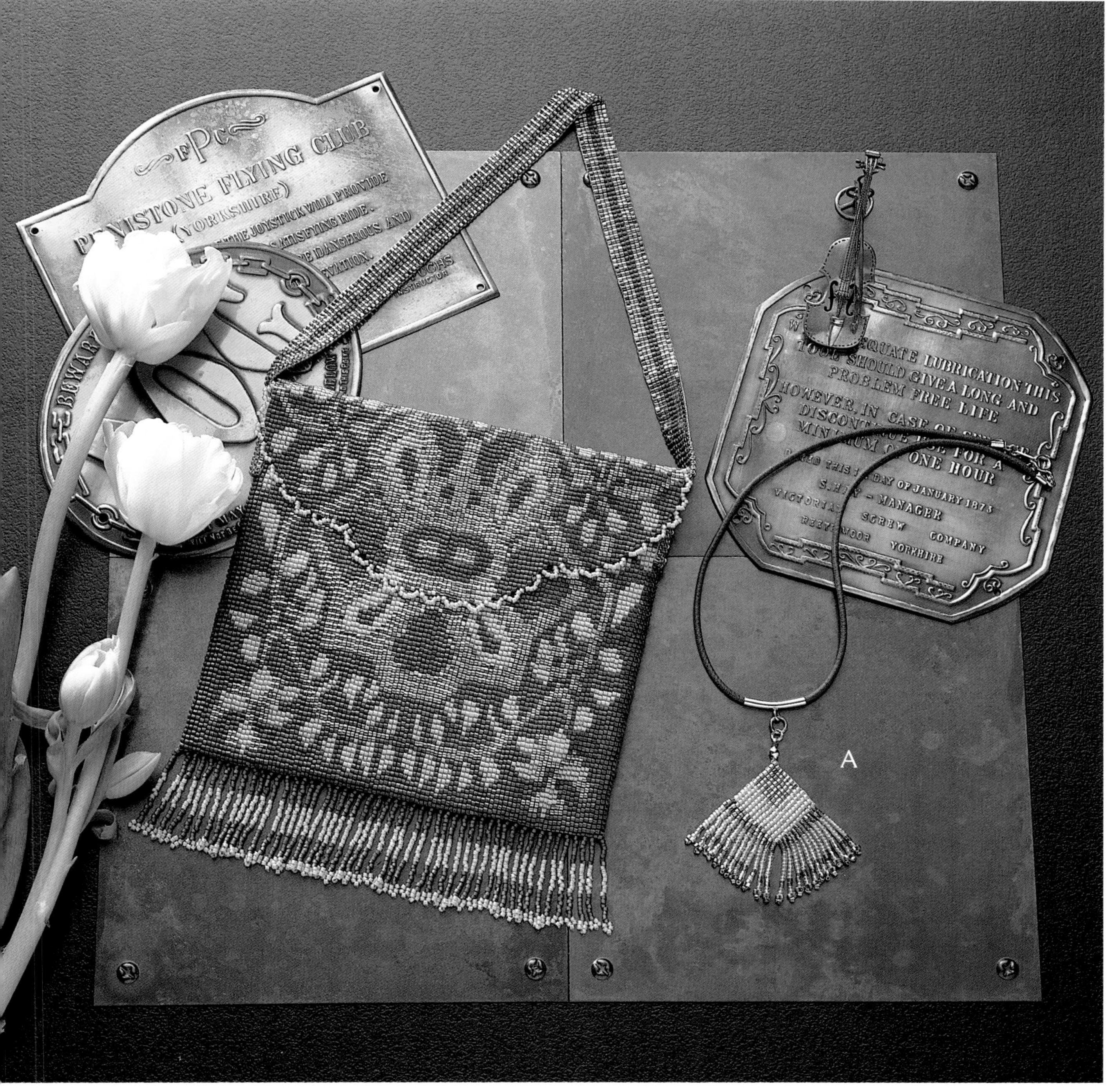

Emblem
Instructions on page 94

A stylish emblem sparkling on the pocket of a blazer coat combines various styles of initials, and heraldry.

Emblems & Small Articles for Personal Adornment

Polka Dotted Ribbon (A)
Instructions on page 101

Ribbon Decoration (B)
Instructions on page 102

Rose Brooch (A)
Instructions on page 105

Nodding in a Gentle Breeze

Money Pouch (A)
Instructions on page 103

Brooch (B)
Instructions on page 103

Making-up Time

Total Fashion

Corsage (A)
Instructions on page 106

Bracelet (B)
Instructions on page 106

Earring (C)
Instructions on page 106

Pouch (D)
Instructions on page 106

C
A
D
B

Star Ribbon (A)
Instructions on page 107

Venetian Glass

Buds are designed to embellish and compliment the roundness of the hem of the bag.

Corsage and star brooch are coordinated in the imagery of the lovely glitter of crystal Venetian glass.

Chain Belt (A)
Instructions on page 108

Personal Party

Gorgeous Aroma

A necklace well-arranged with fringes, a money pouch in gold color and earrings in the form of paper lanterns - a combination of modern and traditional forms.

Paper Lantern Pendant (A)
Instructions on page 109

A
B

As a Guest

Arrangement in silver tone, matching to a pearl gray blouse of silk. A party bag in silver color will swing gently and make a striking impression with its abundant fringes.

Earring (A)
Instructions on page 110

Bracelet (B)
Instructions on page 110

Rhythmical Paisley

The paisley pattern in the form of MAGA-TAMA is the symbol for "Bring Happiness" and is often adopted as a textile pattern. It is possible to modify the rhythmical design by varying it's direction and size.

Brooch (A)
Instructions on page 111

Ethnic Style

Money Pouch (A)
Instructions on page 113

Small Case (B)
Instructions on page 113

B

Designed for Autumn

Personalized accessories with your initials.

The brooch is one motif and the belt is a continuous repeat of the motif.

Initialed Pouch (A)
Instructions on page 92

Brooch (B)
Instructions on page 113

Belt (C)
Instructions on page 113

Classic Concert

A

B

Handbag (A)
Instructions on page 114

Bracelet (B)
Instructions on page 114

A

Reticule
The center section is in sepia color and the background is in nickel color, with many small and large arranged roses. The panel is woven sideways and finished without an end.
Finished size: 19.5cm x 23cm

Antique

Elegant design in French style with repeat rose pattern

Evening Glow

A delicate Oriental rose pattern with a 19th c. frame, captures an antique aire.

Handbag

Instructions on page 118

B
A

Lavender

The memory of lavender from a journey is captured with beads.

Brooch (A)
Instructions on page 122
Handbag (B)
Instructions on page 122
Belt (C)
Instructions on page 122

Variations

Handbag

Change the combination of colors on the same pattern, and the mood will be changed. With this fine classic design brown beads are used for quiet and stylish adornment, pink beads are used for holidays and a silver pouch will enhance dress clothes.

Finishing size: about 17cm x 28cm

COLOR COMBINATIONS
From the left side:

BROWN BAG
Frosted brown (TB702)
Nickel (TB711)
Dark brown (TB83)

PINK BAG
Silver (TB558)
Nickel (TB711)
Orange (TB779)

GRAY BAG
Picots enhance the top exposed edge of this draw string bag.
Silver (TB558)
Nickel (TB711)
Charcoal gray (TB81)

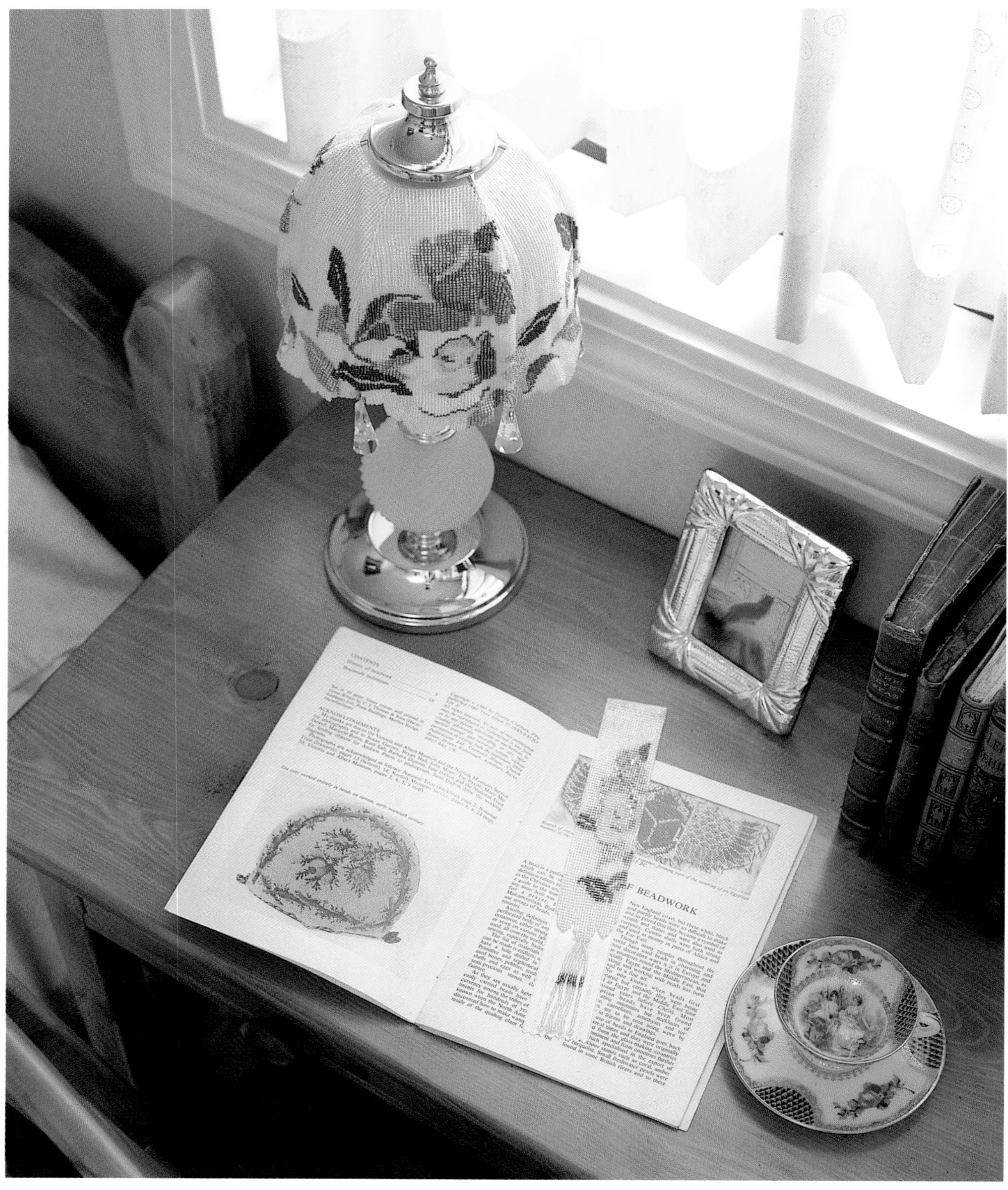

Bookmark
Instructions on page 123

Peaceful Time

BEAD WEAVING BASICS

See Appendix, Pg 112 for a two needle alternate weaving technique, a preferred method for wide weaving and when weaving complex patterns.

Warping

Warp threads should have uniform tension with loom adjustment for control of tension. When weaving is not in progress, tension should be relaxed.

Terminating Weft

Tie weft thread with a double knot to a warp thread, pass through a bead and cut off at the end of the panel.

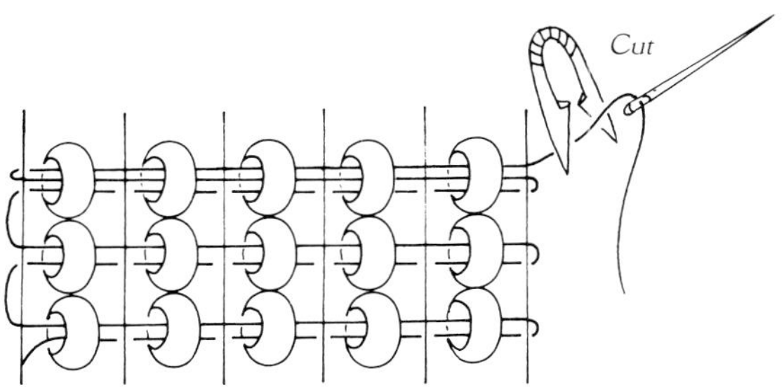

Terminating Warp

Pass each warp thread through a needle and run it through wefts between beads, one-by-one.

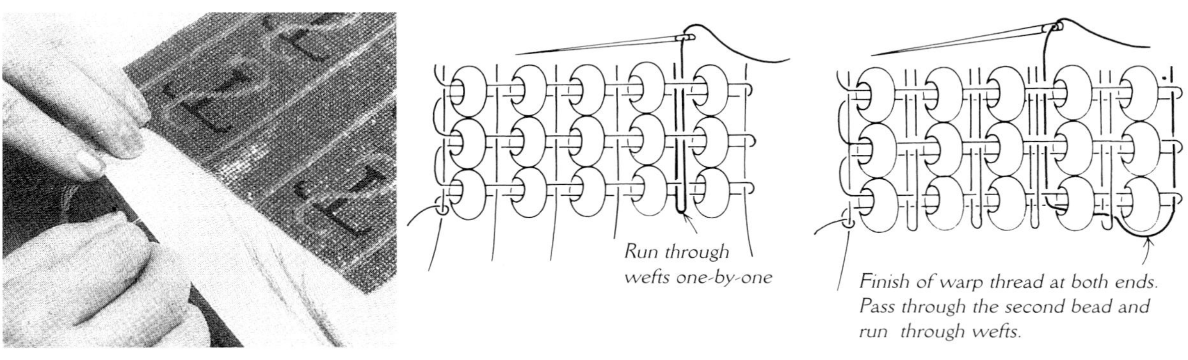

Run through wefts one-by-one
Finish of warp thread at both ends. Pass through the second bead and run through wefts.

Drawing Warp Threads

Remove panel from loom and fix with tape. Divide warp, right and left from center and draw thread up and down alternately.

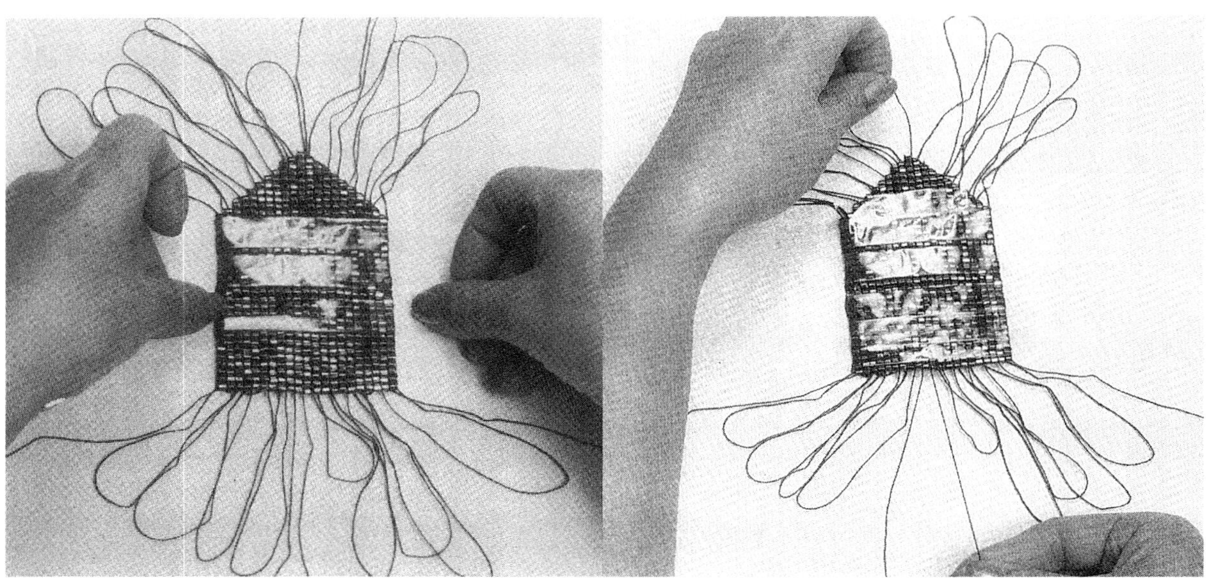

1. Fix panel with tape.

2. Draw from center, warp threads up and down alternately in order.

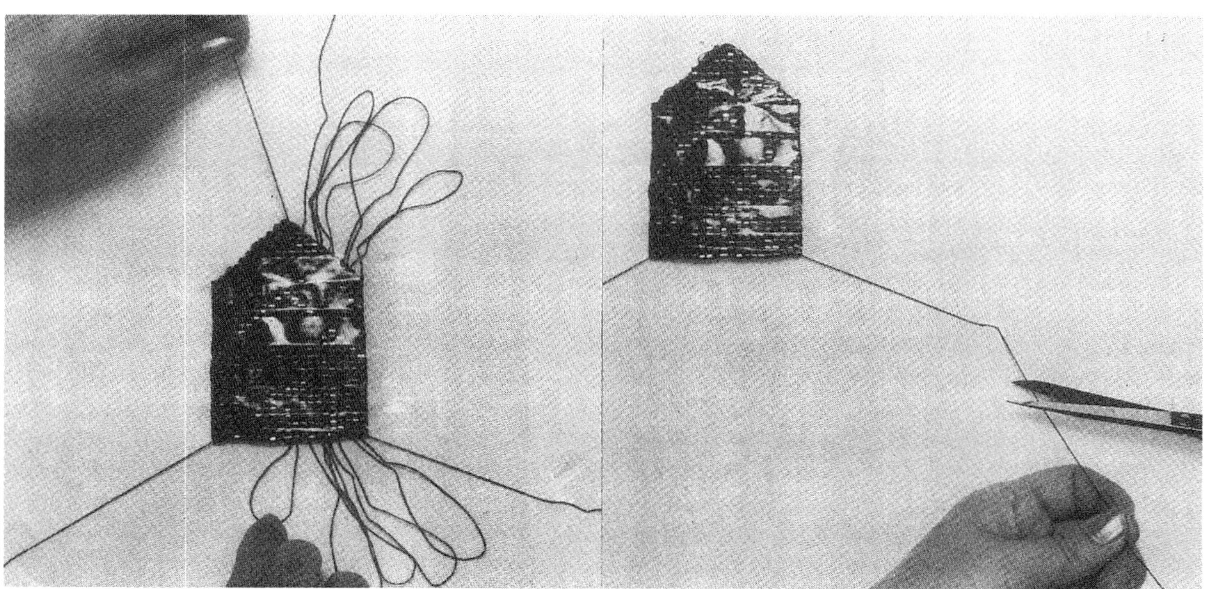

3. When left half is finished, draw thread on right half.

4. Pass the last thread through needle and finish

FRINGE WEAVING INSTRUCTIONS

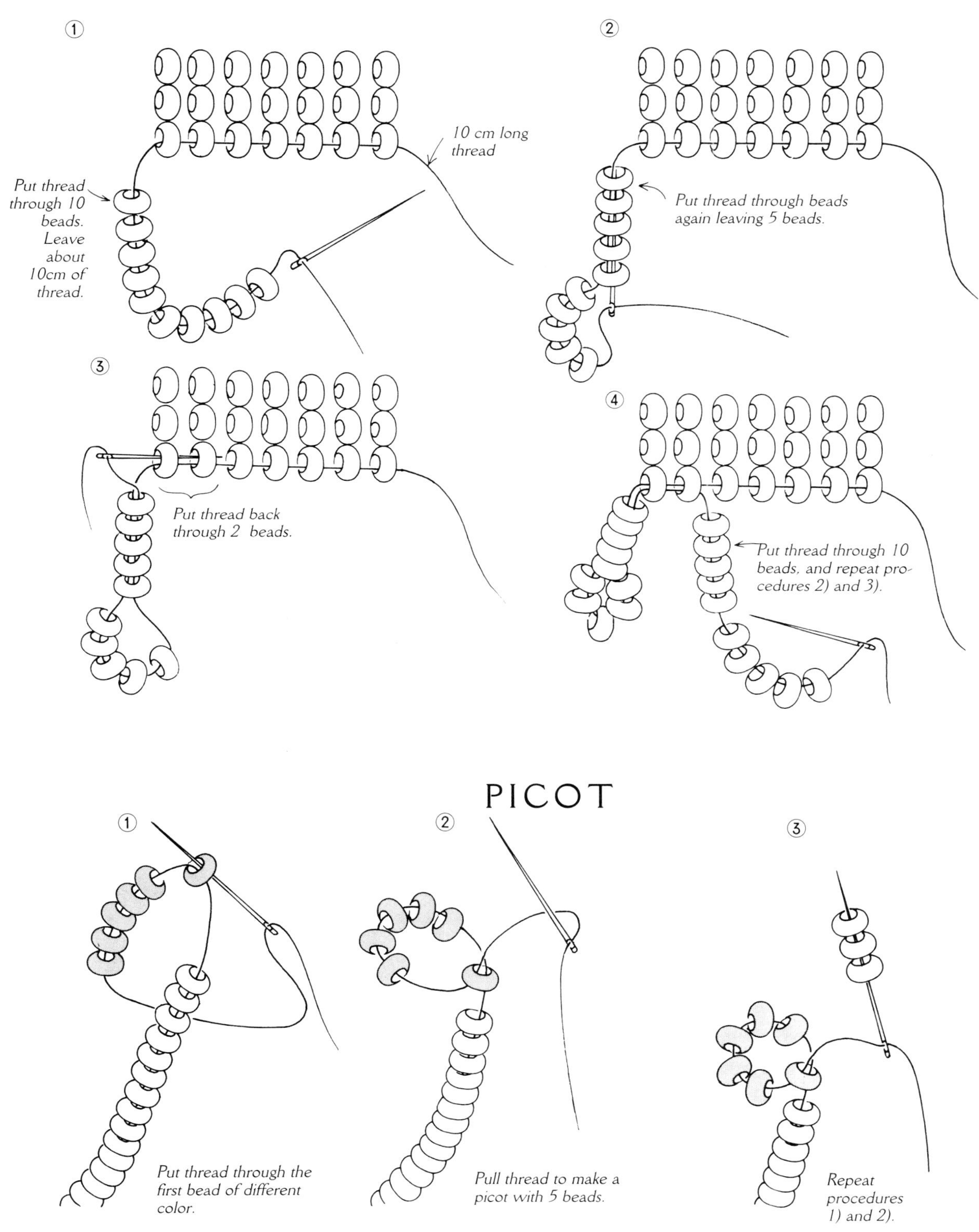

①
10 cm long thread
Put thread through 10 beads. Leave about 10cm of thread.
②
Put thread through beads again leaving 5 beads.
③
Put thread back through 2 beads.
④
Put thread through 10 beads, and repeat procedures 2) and 3).
PICOT
①
Put thread through the first bead of different color.
②
Pull thread to make a picot with 5 beads.
③
Repeat procedures 1) and 2).

PINEAPPLE FORMED FRINGE

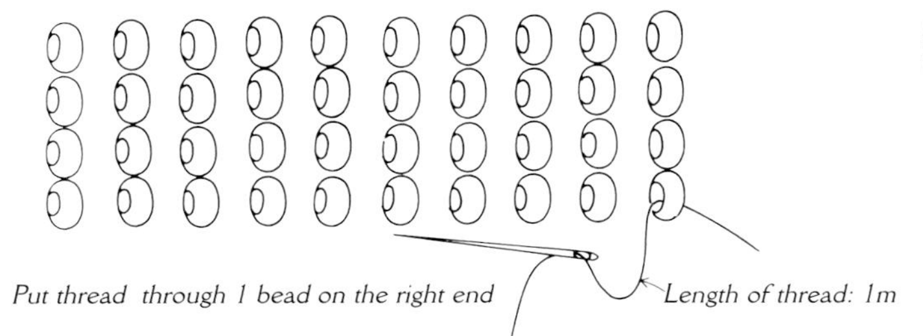

Put thread through 1 bead on the right end
Length of thread: 1m

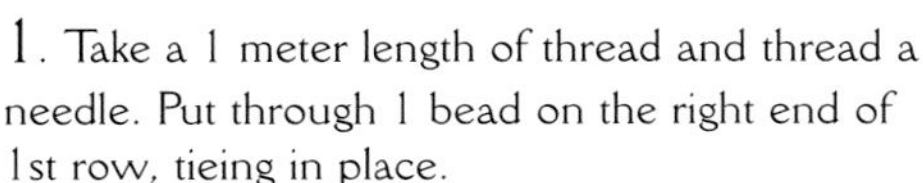

1. Take a 1 meter length of thread and thread a needle. Put through 1 bead on the right end of 1st row, tieing in place.

2. Thread 7 beads (must be an odd number) and put thread through the 4th bead in bottom row (skipping 3 beads).

3. Repeat procedure shown in Picture 2, making loops to the left end.

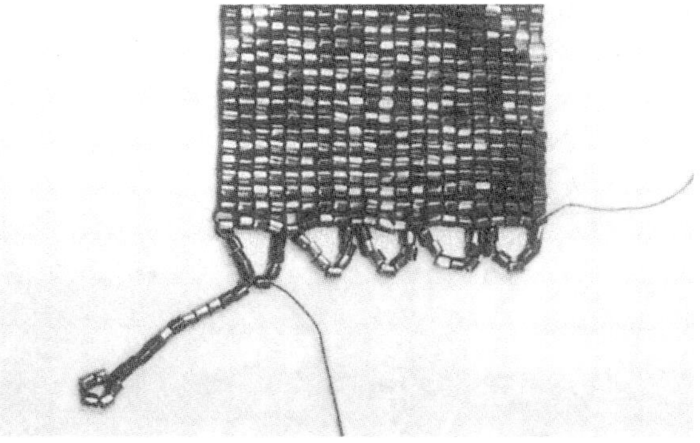

4. Return to middle bead of the end loop, and make one strand of fringe with picot.

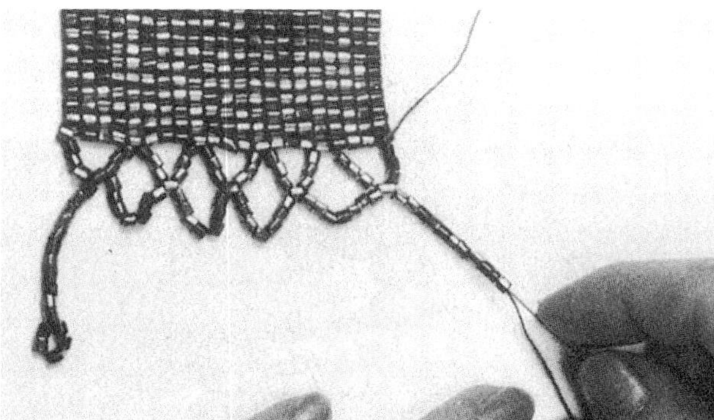

5. Put thread through center bead of loop, and make a another loop with 7 beads shown.

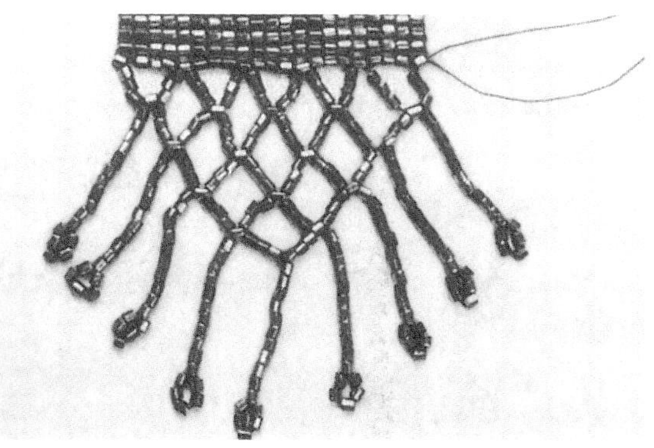

6. Proceed making and attaching fringes on the right and left sides. Finish after attaching a fringe at the mid-point.

Window Pendant

Pictured on page 9

● MATERIALS

Beads . . . . Dark Blue 5g, Light Blue 3g, Pink 1g
Thread . . . . .Gray
Horizontal x Vertical rows . . . . .25 x 23
Number of Threads 26
Fringe . . . . .26 strands

FRINGE

String 40 Dark Blue Beads and 6 Pink Beads and repeat.

STITCH CHART

Figures at left of each row indicate row number.

Figures on horizontal lines show number of stitches for designated bead.

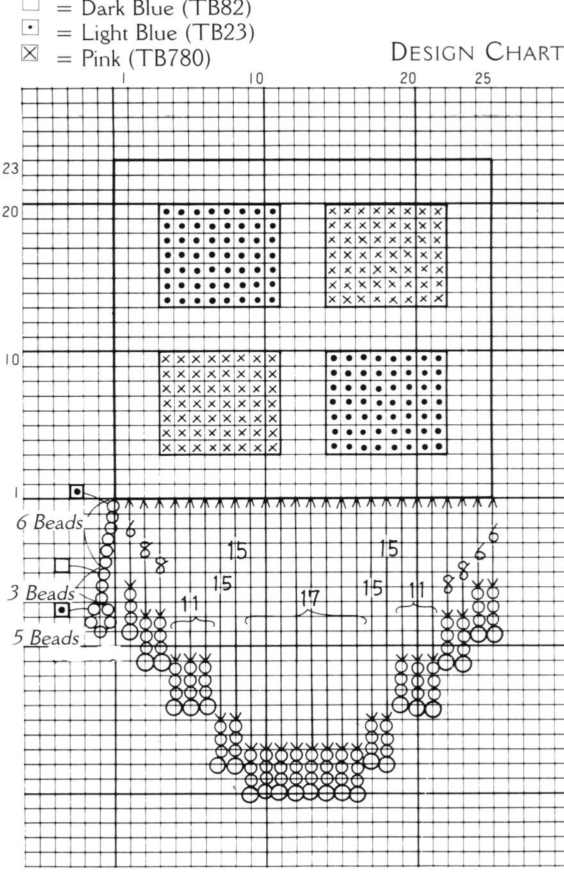

Stitch Chart

1	25			
2	25			
3	25			
4	3	8×	3	8●	3
5	3	8×	3	8●	3
6	3	8×	3	8●	3
7	3	8×	3	8●	3
8	3	8×	3	8●	3
9	3	8×	3	8●	3
10	3	8×	3	8●	3
11	25				
12	25				
13	25				
14	3	8●	3	8×	3
15	3	8●	3	8×	3
16	3	8●	3	8×	3
17	3	8●	3	8×	3
18	3	8●	3	8×	3
19	3	8●	3	8×	3
20	3	8●	3	8×	3
21	25				
22	25				
23	25				

Fringe

Thread			
1	6●	3	5●
2	6●	3	5●
3	8●	3	5●
4	8●	3	5●
5	11●	3	5●
6	11●	3	5●
7	11●	3	5●
8	15●	3	5●
9	15●	3	5●
10	17●	3	5●
11	17●	3	5●
12	17●	3	5●
13	17●	3	5●

Fit fringes from 1st to 13th threads and return from 13th to 1st thread, 26 lines in total.

Diamond Pendant

Pictured on page 8

● MATERIALS

Beads . . . . Gold 3g, Nickel 3g
Thread . . . . Gray
Supplies . . . . Gold Chain Set
Horizontal x Vertical rows . . . . 25 x 25
Number of Threads 26
Fringe . . . . 26 beads x 26 strands

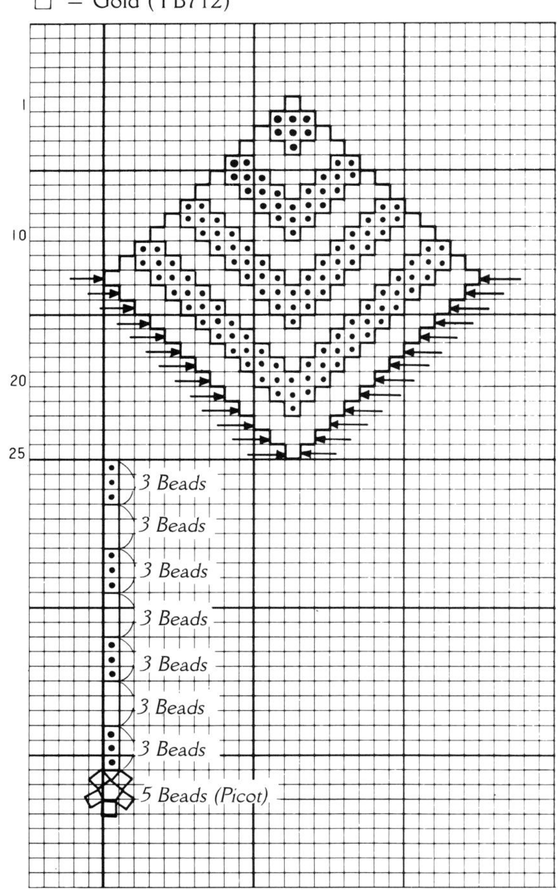

Weave from 25th row to 1st row

Row									
1	1								
2	3●								
3	1	3●	1						
4	3	1●	3						
5	2●	5	2●						
6	1	3●	3	3●	1				
7	3	3●	1	3●	3				
8	2●	3	5●	3	2●				
9	1	3●	3	3●	3	3●	1		
10	3	3●	3	1●	3	3●	3		
11	2●	3	3●	5	3●	3	2●		
12	1	3●	3	3●	3	3●	3	3●	1
13	3	3●	3	3●	1	3●	3	3●	3
14	3	3●	3	5●	3	3●	3		
15	3	3●	3	3●	3	3●	3		
16	3	3●	3	1●	3	3●	3		
17	3	3●	5	3●	3				
18	3	3●	3	3●	3				
19	3	3●	1	3●	3				
20	3	5●	3						
21	3	3●	3						
22	3	1●	3						
23	5								
24	3								
25	1								

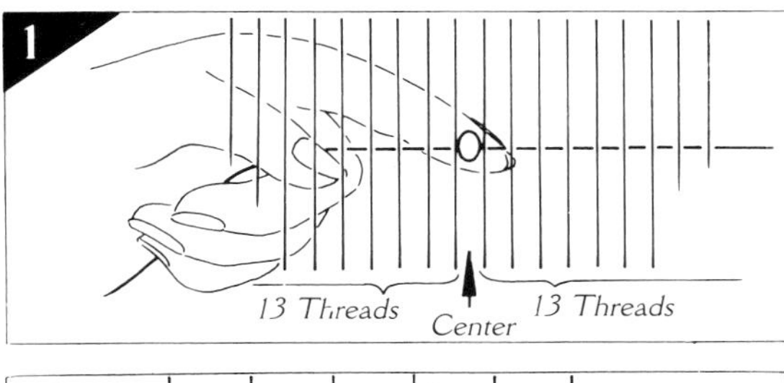

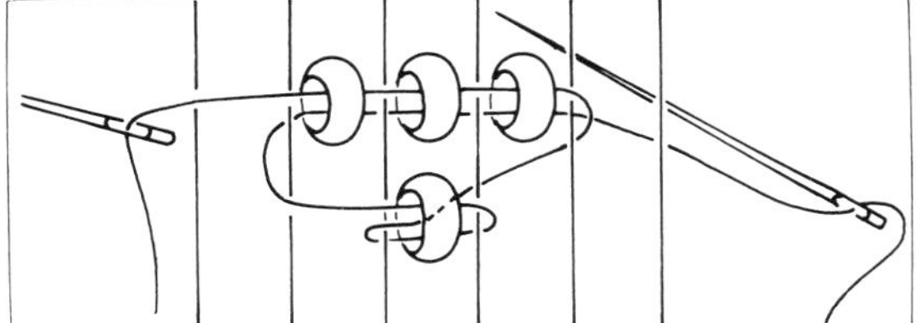

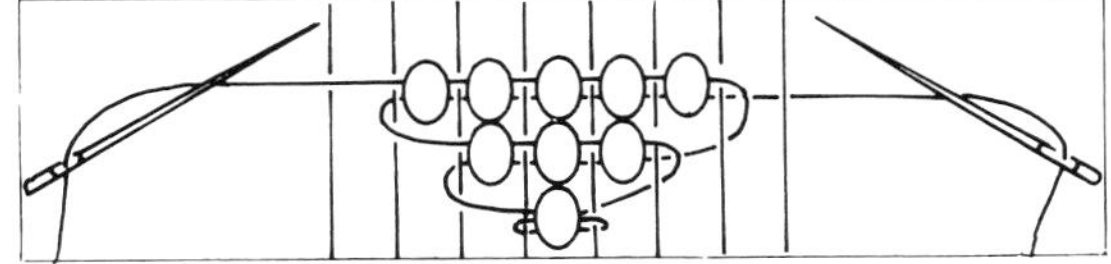

Put each end of weft through a needle, and cross threads in beads to secure them.

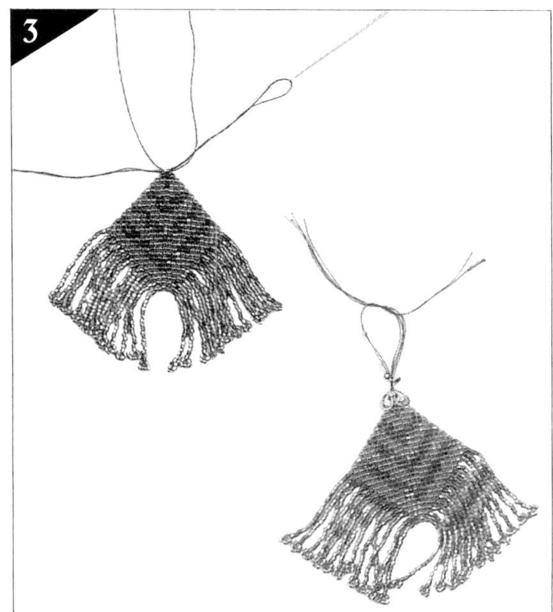

After finishing and fitting fringe, fit metal finding on the end of panel.

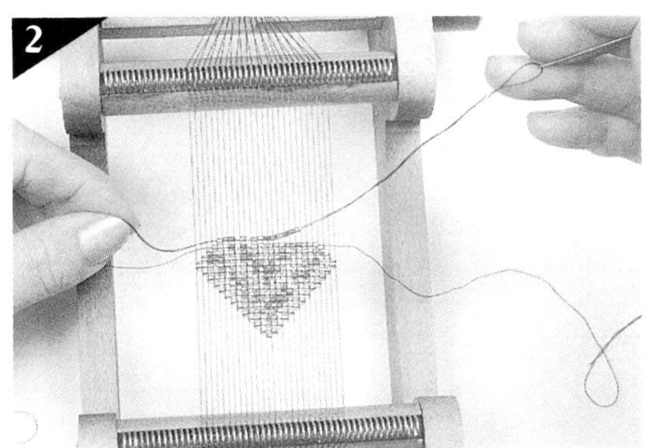

Reduce the number of stitches from 14th row.

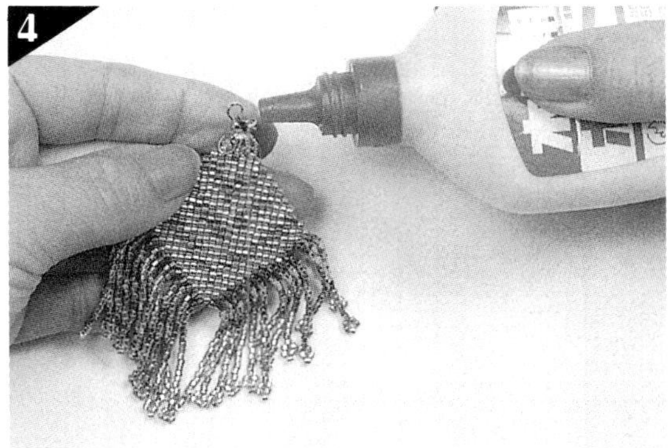

Secure it with a knot in thread and glue

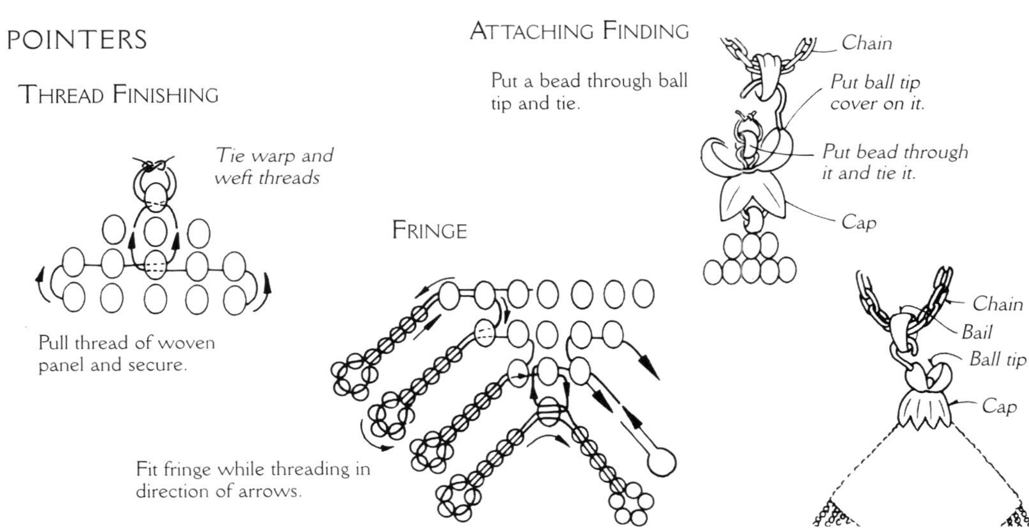

POINTERS

Thread Finishing

Pull thread of woven panel and secure.

Attaching Finding

Put a bead through ball tip and tie.

Fringe

Fit fringe while threading in direction of arrows.

Family Rose Necklace

Pictured on page 11

● MATERIALS

Beads . . Ivory 24g, Green 3g, Purplish Red 3g
Pink 3g, Yellow Green 3g, Wine Red 3g
Thread . . . . Beige
Supplies . . . . Gold Chain Set
Horizontal x Vertical rows . . . . 16 x 121
Number of Threads . . . . 18 x 80cm
Fringe . . . . 26 beads x 26strands

□ = Ivory (TB122)
⊠ = Green (TB507)
⊙ = Purplish Red (TB785)
● = Pink (TB780)
⊡ = Yellow Green (TB775)
△ = Wine Red (TB332)

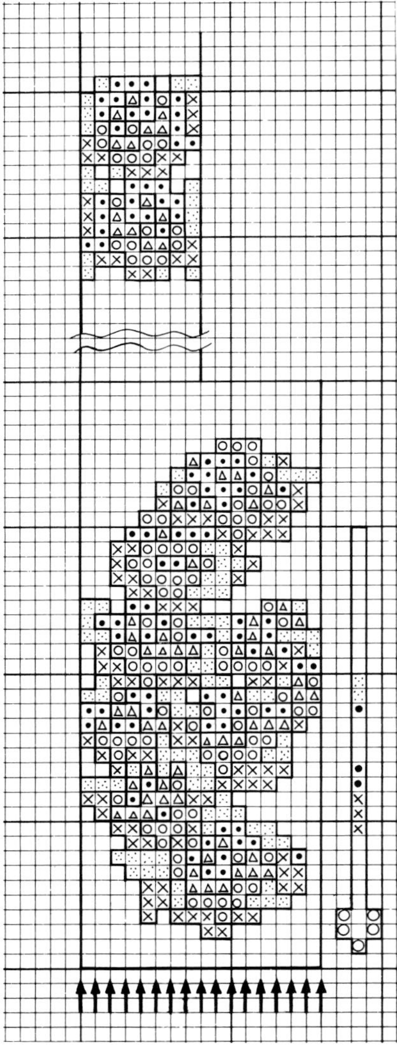

Row													
1	16												
2	16												
3	8	2×	6										
4	4	1×	1	3×	1○	2×	4						
5	4	2×	1⊡	4○	3⊡	2							
6	4	2×	1⊡	3△	2○	1⊡	2×	1					
7	3	3⊡	1○	1△	2●	3△	2×	1					
8	2	4⊡	1○	1●	1△	1●	1○	1△	1○	1×	1●	1	
9	3	2×	1○	1×	1○	1●	1△	2●	2⊡	2			
10	2	2×	3○	1×	1⊡	2●	2⊡	3					
11	1	1×	3△	1●	2○	3⊡	5						
12	2×	1○	1●	3△	2×	1⊡	6						
13	3⊡	1△	1●	1△	1○	2⊡	4×	3					
14	2	1×	1⊡	1△	1⊡	1△	2⊡	1○	4×	2			
15	1	1×	1○	2×	3⊡	4○	2⊡	2					
16	1×	4○	1⊡	2×	3△	2○	1⊡	2					
17	1●	1△	2●	2△	1×	1○	2●	1○	3△	1×	1		
18	2●	2△	1●	1○	2⊡	1○	2●	1○	2●	2○			
19	2⊡	1○	2●	2⊡	1	2●	1△	2⊡	1○	2△			
20	1	1⊡	2×	1○	3×	2⊡	1	2×	1⊡	1△	1○		
21	1	2×	4○	2⊡	4○	1×	2●						
22	1	1×	2○	4△	1⊡	1○	1△	1●	1△	1●	1×	1⊡	
23	2⊡	1●	1△	1●	1△	1○	2●	1⊡	1●	1△	2●	3⊡	
24	1⊡	2●	1△	1○	1●	1○	3	1●	1△	1●	1○	1△	1
25	2⊡	1	2●	3×	4	1○	1△	1⊡	1				
26	3	2×	2○	3⊡	6								
27	2	2×	4○	2⊡	1×	5							
28	2	1×	2○	2●	1△	1○	2⊡	1×	4				
29	2	2×	4○	2⊡	1×	5							
30	3	2●	1△	3●	1×	1○	3×	2					
31	4	2○	3×	3○	2×	2							
32	5	1×	1△	1●	1△	1●	1○	1△	2○	1×	1		
33	5	1⊡	2○	3●	1○	1△	1●	1×	1				
34	6	1⊡	2●	2△	1●	1○	3⊡						
35	7	1△	3●	1○	1⊡	1×	2						
36	9	3○	4										
37	16												
38	16												
39	16												
40	16												

BAND: LEFT							
41	8						
∫							
67	8						
68	1⊡	2	2×	1⊡	1	1⊡	
69	1⊡	2×	3○	2×			
70	2●	2○	2△	1○	1×		
71	1×	1●	2△	1○	1●	1○	1⊡
72	1×	1●	1△	2●	1△	1●	1⊡
73	1×	1●	1○	1●	1△	2●	1⊡
74	2⊡	1	3●	1	1⊡		
75	1⊡	1	1⊡	3×	2		
76	2×	3○	2×	1			
77	1×	1○	2△	2○	2●		
78	1⊡	1○	1●	1○	2△	1●	1×
79	1⊡	1●	1△	2●	1△	1●	1×
80	1⊡	2●	1△	1●	1○	1●	1×
81	1	1⊡	3●	1	2⊡		
82	8						
∫							
121	8						

BAND: RIGHT							
41	8						
∫							
67	8						
68	1⊡	1	1⊡	2×	2	1⊡	
69	2×	3○	2×	1⊡			
70	1×	1○	2△	2○	2●		
71	1⊡	1○	1●	1○	2△	1●	1×
72	1⊡	1●	1△	2●	1△	1●	1×
73	1⊡	2●	1△	1●	1○	1●	1×
74	1⊡	1	3●	1	2⊡		
75	2	3×	1⊡	1	1⊡		
76	1	2×	3○	2×			
77	2●	2○	2△	1○	1×		
78	1×	1●	2△	1○	1●	1○	1⊡
79	1×	1●	1△	2●	1△	1●	1⊡
80	1×	1●	1○	1●	1△	2●	1⊡
81	2⊡	1	3●	1⊡	1		
82	8						
∫							
121	8						

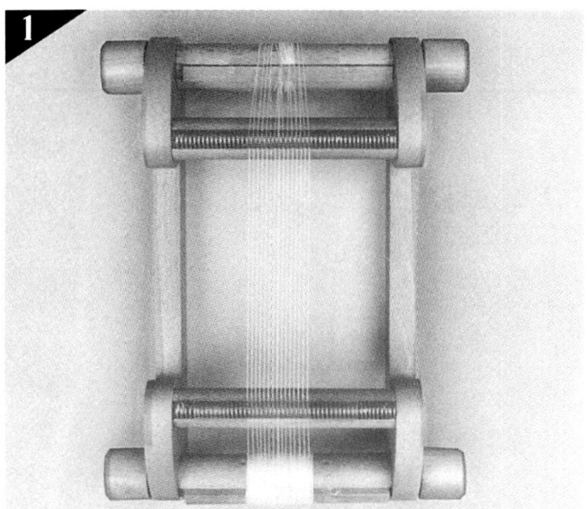

Prepare 18 warp threads in 17 lines with double warp at center.

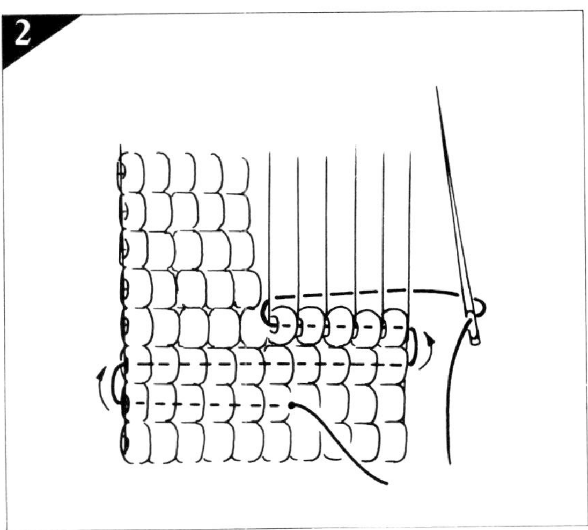

Secure new weft and weave on both sides respectively.

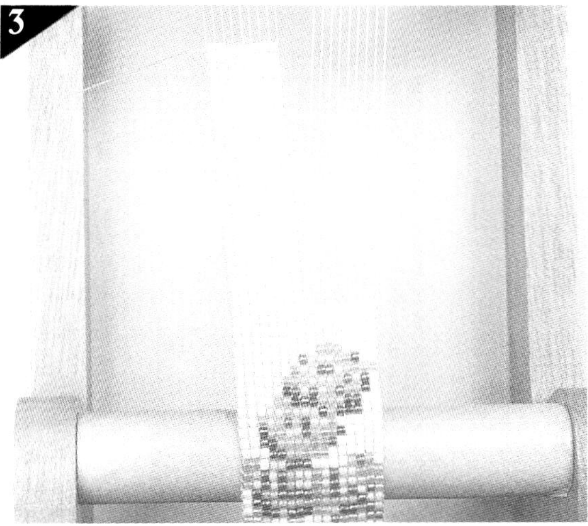

Weave threads on right and left sides while rotating panel.

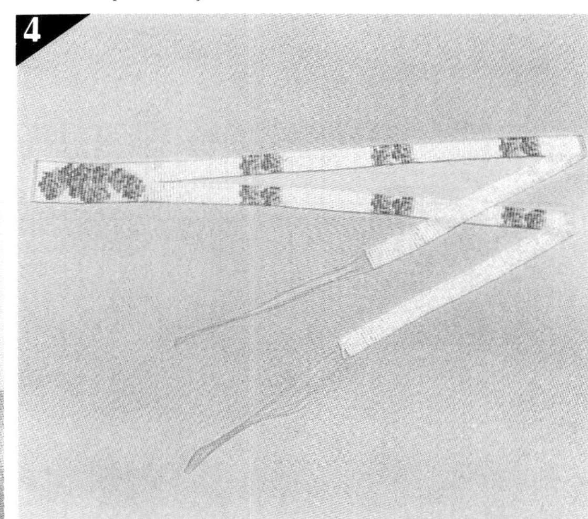

Remove panel from loom and finish pendant section.

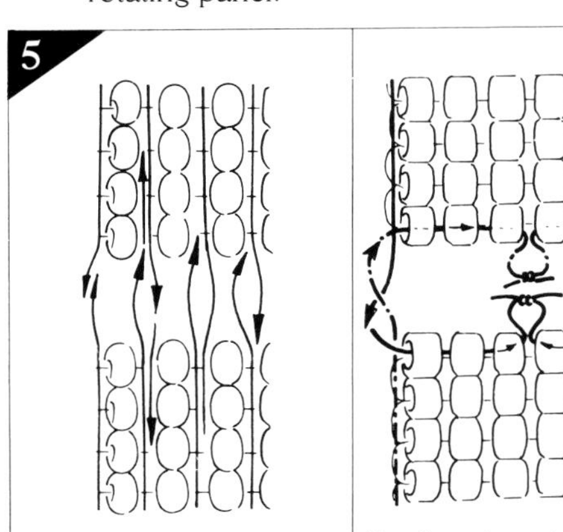

Terminate warp after passing it through weft threads on opposite side.

Put threads on both sides through beads on the opposite side, and tie at the center.

Match threads on both sides of each other, put warp through panel on one side respectively, and tie them together.

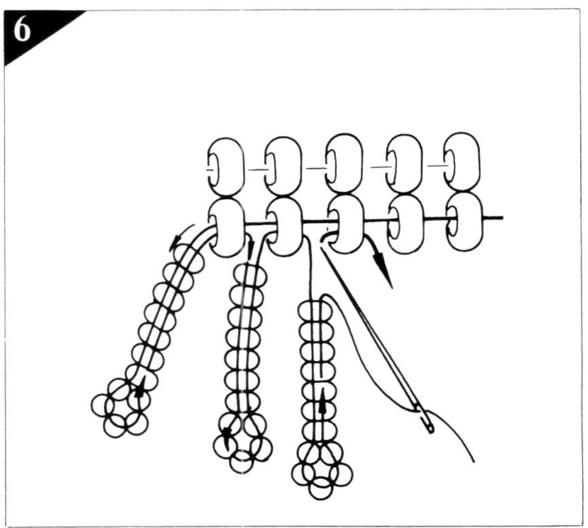

Make 17 lines of fringe, tie it to end threads and finish working.

Camel Brooch

Pictured on page 9

● MATERIALS

Beads . . . . Dark Blue 6g, Nickel 3g, Gold, 3g
Thread . . . . .Black
Supplies . . . . .Gold Brooch Pin Back
Horizontal x Vertical rows . . . . .31 x 36
Number of Threads 32

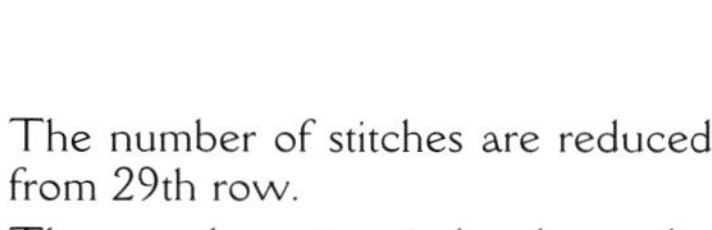

The number of stitches are reduced from 29th row.

The numbers in circle show the number of stitches to be reduced.

□ = Dark Blue (TB82)
⊡ = Gold (TB712)
⊠ = Nickel (TB711)

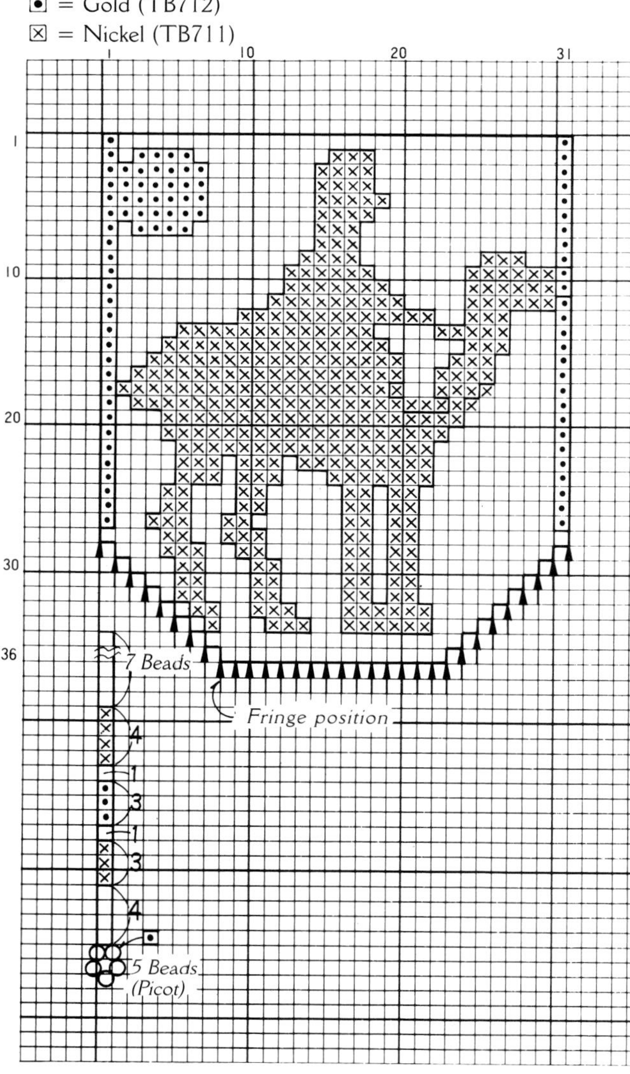

1	1●	29	1●								
2	1●	1	4●	9	3×	12	1●				
3	7●	7	4×	12	1●						
4	7●	7	4×	12	1●						
5	7●	7	5×	11	1●						
6	7●	7	4×	12	1●						
7	1●	1	4●	8	3×	13	1●				
8	1●	13	3×	13	1●						
9	1●	12	4×	8	3×	2	1●				
10	1●	11	6×	6	6×	1●					
11	1●	11	7×	5	6×	1●					
12	1●	10	9×	4	6×	1●					
13	1●	8	13×	2	3×	3	1●				
14	1●	4	13×	4	5×	3	1●				
15	1●	3	15×	5	3×	3	1●				
16	1●	2	17×	3	3×	4	1●				
17	1●	1	18×	2	4×	4	1●				
18	1●	19×	2	4×	4	1●					
19	1●	1	23×	5	1●						
20	1●	3	20×	6	1●						
21	1●	3	19×	7	1●						
22	1●	4	17×	8	1●						
23	1●	4	3×	1	3×	1	9×	8	1●		
24	1●	4	3×	1	3×	3	7×	8	1●		
25	1●	3	2×	3	2×	5	2×	1	2×	9	1●
26	1●	3	2×	3	2×	5	2×	1	2×	9	1●
27	1●	2	3×	2	2×	6	2×	1	2×	9	1●
28	4	2×	2	3×	5	2×	1	2×	10		
29	①	3	3×	2	2×	5	2×	1	2×	9	①
30	②	3	2×	3	2×	4	2×	1	2×	8	②
31	③	2	2×	3	2×	4	2×	1	2×	7	③
32	④	1	2×	3	2×	4	2×	1	2×	6	④
33	⑤	1	2×	2	3×	3	6×	4	⑤		
34	⑥	1	1×	3	3×	2	6×	3	⑥		
35	⑦	17	⑦								
36	⑧	15	⑧								

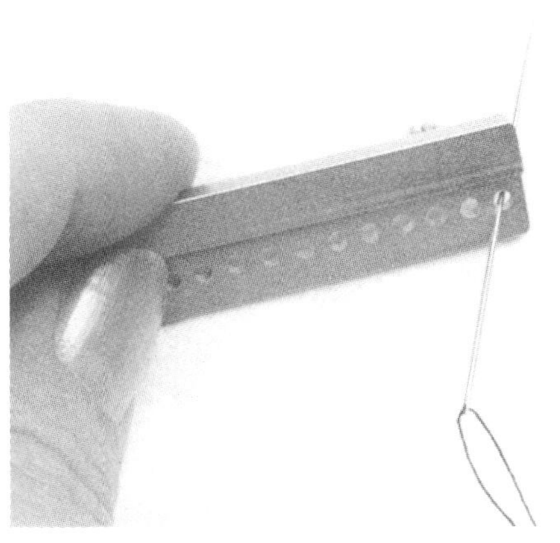

Double a 60cm long thread, put it through right end hole of Pin Back from the face side, leaving 10cm of thread.

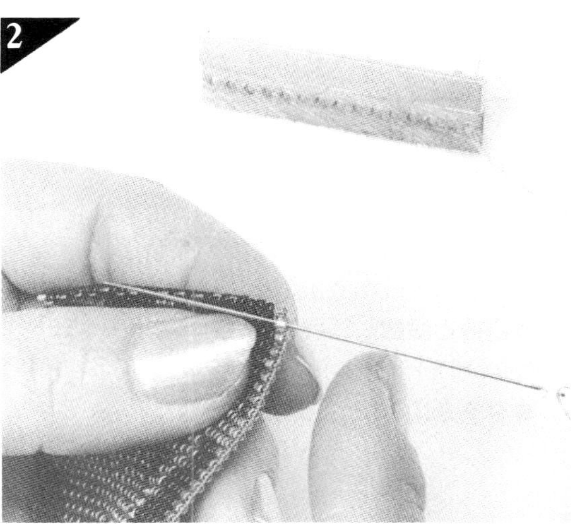

Catch a bead on the right end of 2nd row of panel and put it through the same hole again.

Put it through the 2nd hole of Pin Back and come out to the panel catching two beads and repeat the procedure.

After finishing to the left end, return to the right end reversing procedure.

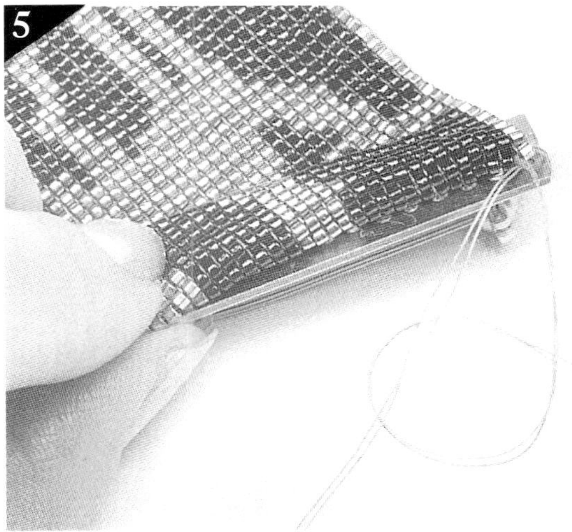

Tie left thread end twice, and finish.

Rose Belt

Pictured on page 17

● MATERIALS

Beads . . . . Nickel 20g, Gold 15g, Silver 13g
Thread . . . . .Gray
Supplies . . . . .Gold Buckle
Horizontal x Vertical rows . . . . .15 x 435
Warp Length . .Waist size + 30cm + 4cm (buckle)

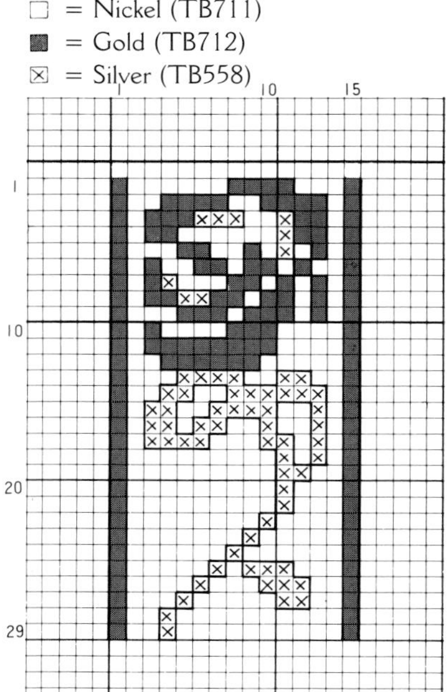

= Nickel (TB711)
● = Gold (TB712)
× = Silver (TB558)

1	1●	6	4●	3	1●							
2	1●	2	4●	2	4●	1	1●					
3	1●	1	3●	3×	2	1×	2●	1	1●			
4	1●	1	2●	6	1×	2●	1	1●				
5	1●	3	2●	2	1●	1	1×	1	1●	1	1●	
6	1●	1	1●	2	2●	1	2●	1	1●	2	1●	
7	1●	1	1●	1×	3	2●	1	1●	1	1●	1	1●
8	1●	1	2●	2×	2●	1	2●	1	1●	1	1●	
9	1●	3	3●	1	3●	1	1●	1	1●			
10	1●	1	1●	4	3●	4	1●					
11	1●	1	8●	4	1●							
12	1●	2	6●	5	1●							
13	1●	3	4×	2	2×	2	1●					
14	1●	2	2×	2	6×	1	1●					
15	1●	1	2×	2	4×	2	1×	1	1●			
16	1●	1	2×	1	2×	2	1×	2	1×	1	1●	
17	1●	1	4×	3	2×	1	1×	1	1●			
18	1●	9	1×	1	1×	1	1●					
19	1●	9	2×	2	1●							
20	1●	9	1×	3	1●							
21	1●	9	1×	3	1●							
22	1●	8	1×	4	1●							
23	1●	7	1×	5	1●							
24	1●	6	1×	6	1●							
25	1●	5	1×	1	3×	3	1●					
26	1●	4	1×	3	3×	2	1●					
27	1●	3	1×	5	2×	2	1●					
28	1●	2	1×	10	1●							
29	1●	2	1×	10	1●							

Party Bag (twill pattern)

Pictured on page 16

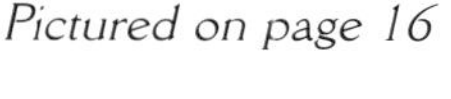

● MATERIALS

Beads . . . Silver 100g, Dark Gold 30g, Red Gold 30g
Thread . . . . Gray
Lining . . . . White Satin, 30cm x 40cm
Supplies . . . . Frame -13cm gold; Chain-1m
Horizontal x Vertical rows . . . . 110 x 115
Thread Length 90cm
Horizontal x Vertical rows . . . . 39 x 41
Number of Threads 111

● HOW TO READ STITCH CHART

The total number of beads on each horizontal line is 110. Following the chart, weave first group, repeat second group 4 times and then weave final group.
For vertical rows, weave 1st through 26th rows, repeating 4 times. Weave 1st through 11th row, completing one side.

STITCH CHART

	1 TIME			REPEAT 4 TIMES																			1 TIME			
1	2			1×	1●	3	1●	1×	3	1×	1●	3	1●	3	1●	1×	5						1×	1●	2	
2	3			1×	1●	3	1●	1×	3	1×	1●	5	1●	1×	7								1×	1●	1	
3	4			1×	1●	3	1●	1×	3	1×	1●	3	1●	1×	3	1×	5						1×	1●		
4	3			1×	1●	5	1●	1×	3	1×	1●	3	1●	1×	1	1×	1●	1×	3				1×	1●	1	
5	1×	1		1×	1●	3	1●	3	1●	1×	3	1×	1●	3	1●	1×	1●	1	1●	1×	1		1×	1●	2	
6	1●	1×		1	1×	1●	1	1●	1×	1●	3	1●	1×	3	1×	1●	3	1●	3	1●	1×		1	1×	1●	1
7	1×			3	1×	1●	1×	1	1×	1●	3	1●	1×	3	1×	1●	5	1●	1×				3	1×	1●	
8				5	1×	3	1×	1●	3	1●	1×	3	1×	1●	3	1●	1×						5	1×		
9	1×			7	1×	1●	5	1●	1×	3	1×	1●	3	1●	1×								5			
10				1●	1×	5	1×	1●	3	1●	3	1●	1×	3	1×	1●	3						1●	1×	4	
11				1×	5	1×	1●	3	1●	1×	1●	3	1●	1×	3	1×	1●	1	1●				1×	5		
12				5	1×	1●	3	1●	1×	1	1×	1●	3	1●	1×	3	1×	1●	1×				5	1×		
13	4			1×	1●	3	1●	1×	3	1×	1●	3	1●	1×	3	1×	5						1×	1●		
14	3			1×	1●	3	1●	1×	3	1×	1●	5	1●	1×	7								1×	1●	1	
15	2			1×	1●	3	1●	1×	3	1×	1●	3	1●	3	1●	1×	5						1×	1●	2	
16	1			1×	1●	3	1●	1×	5	1×	1●	1	1●	1×	1●	1	1●	1×	5				1×	1●	3	
17				1×	1●	3	1●	1×	7	1×	1●	1×	1	1×	1●	1×	5						1×	1●	3	1●
18				1●	3	1●	1×	9	1×	3	1×	5	1×										1●	3	1●	1×
19				3	1●	1×	5	1×	3	1×	9	1×	1●										3	1●	1×	1
20	2			1●	1×	5	1×	1●	1×	1	1×	1●	1×	7	1×	1●	3						1●	1×	2	
21	1			1●	1×	5	1×	1●	1	1●	1×	1●	1	1●	1×	5	1×	1●	3				1●	1×	3	
22				1●	1×	5	1×	1●	3	1●	3	1●	1×	3	1×	1●	3						1●	1×	4	
23				1×	7	1×	1●	5	1●	1×	3	1×	1●	3	1●								1×	5		
24				5	1×	3	1×	1●	3	1●	1×	3	1×	1●	3	1●	1×						5	1×		
25	4			1×	1●	1×	3	1×	1●	3	1●	1×	1	1×	1●	3	1●	1×	5				1×	1●	1●	
26	3			1×	1●	1	1●	1×	3	1×	1●	3	1●	1×	1●	3	1●	1×	5				1×	1●		

□ = Silver (TB558)

⊠ = Dark Gold (TB221)

◘ = Red Gold (TB502)

Design Chart

Terminating Warp Threads

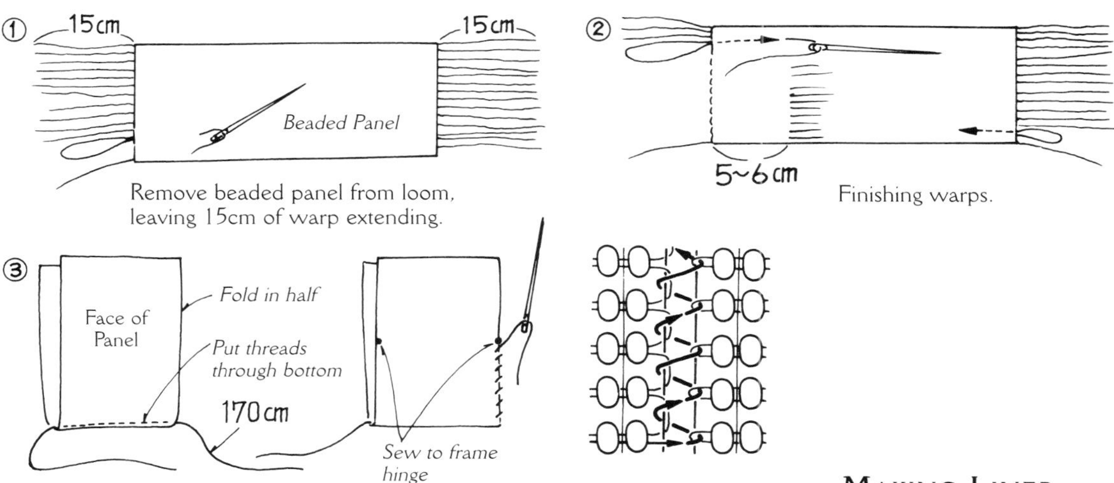

Making Liner

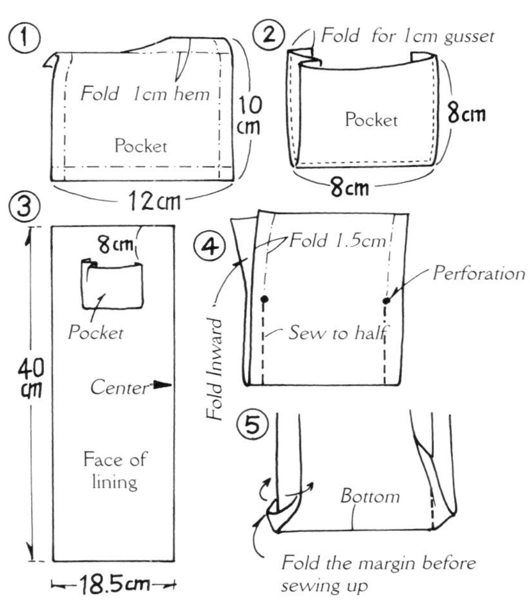

Fringes

Fold panel in half, stitch sides and fit fringe to bottom.

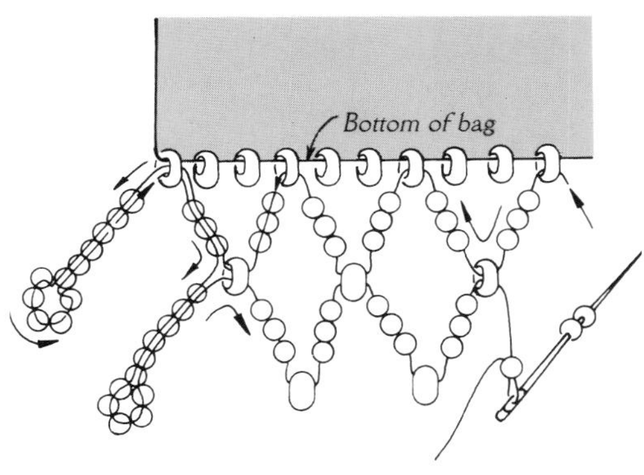

1. Measure the finished panel.
2. Make pocket and sew it on.
3. Sew inner bag with the pocket on the inside.

Fitting Frame

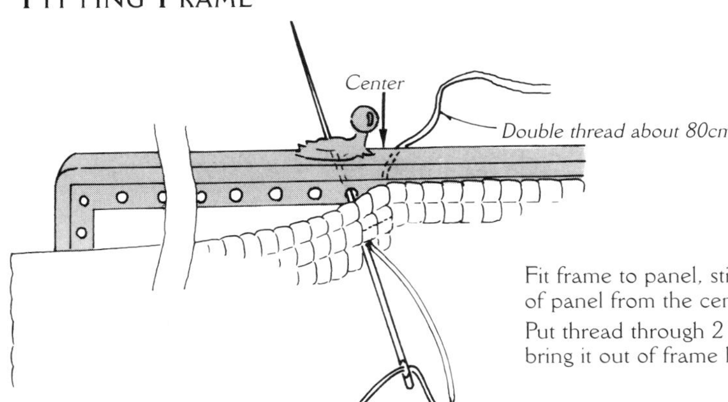

Fit frame to panel, stitching 2nd row of panel from the center to left side.

Put thread through 2 beads, and bring it out of frame hole.

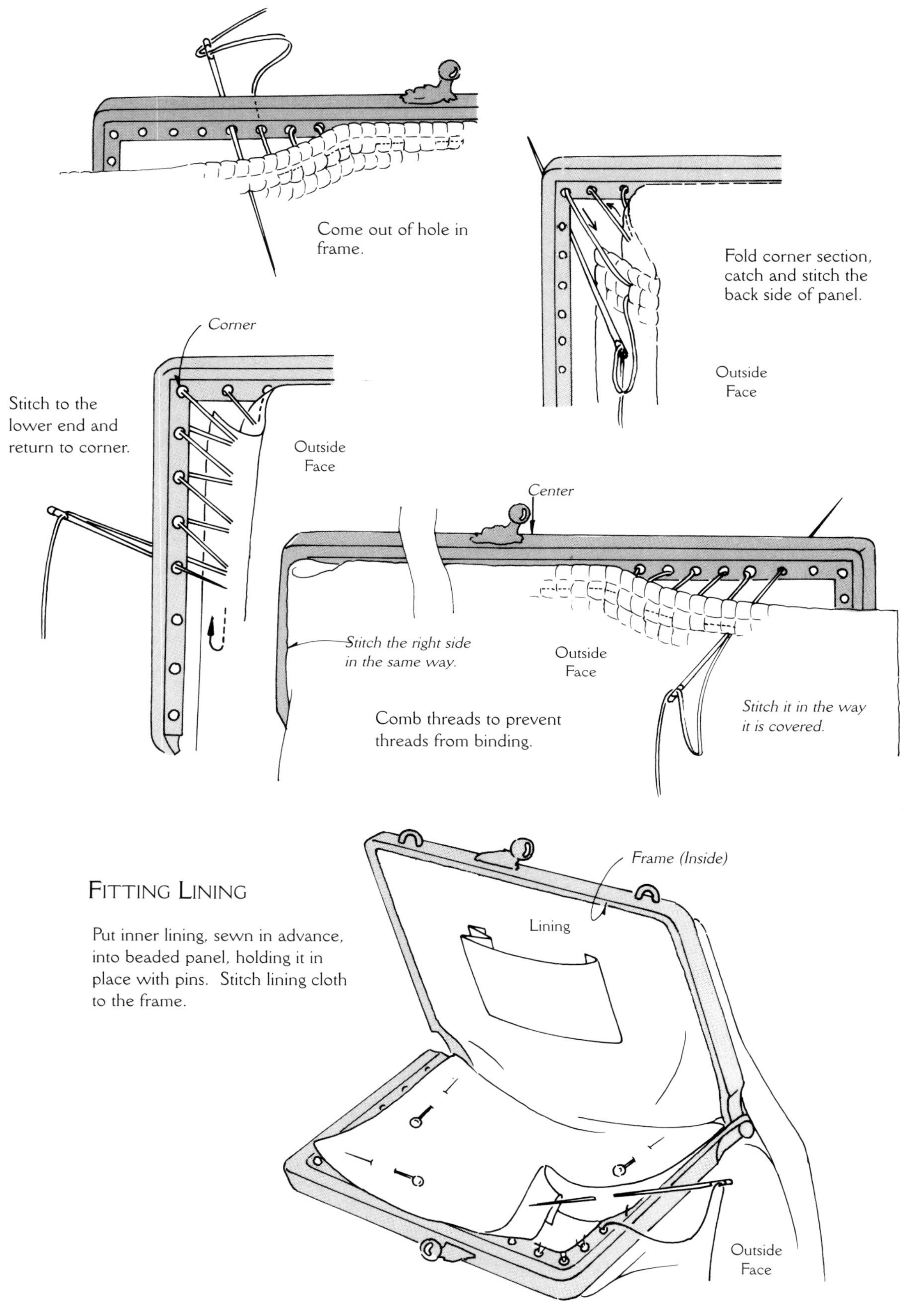

Come out of hole in frame.
Fold corner section, catch and stitch the back side of panel.
Outside Face
Corner
Stitch to the lower end and return to corner.
Outside Face
Center
Stitch the right side in the same way.
Outside Face
Comb threads to prevent threads from binding.
Stitch it in the way it is covered.
Frame (Inside)
Lining
Outside Face

Fitting Lining

Put inner lining, sewn in advance, into beaded panel, holding it in place with pins. Stitch lining cloth to the frame.

Cattleya Brooch

Pictured on page 8

● MATERIALS

Beads . . . . . . Black 3g, Green 1g, Red Gold 1g, Gold 1g, Purplish Red 2g
Thread . . . . Black
Supplies . . . . Ball Tip - Gold
Brooch Frame - 3cm Gold,
Horizontal x Vertical rows 21 x 28
Number of Threads 22

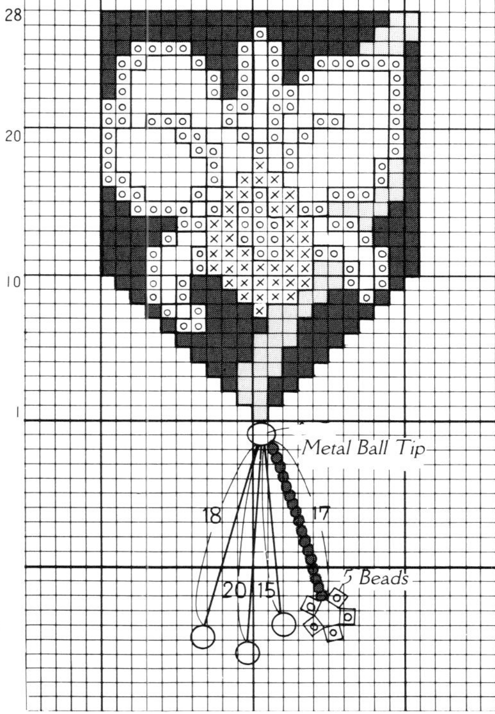

■ = Black (TB49)
⊡ = Gold (TB712)
□ = Purplish Red (TB785)
⊠ = Red Gold (TB222)
□ = Green (TB507)

Flower Pinwheel Brooch

Pictured on page 9

● MATERIALS

Beads . . . . Silver 4g, Gold 4g, Yellow Green 1g, Green 1g, Red 1g, Pink 1g
Thread . . . . Gray
Supplies Brooch Frame - 4.5cm Gold, Ball Tip - Gold
Horizontal x Vertical rows . . . . . . 31 x 31
Number of Warp Threads 32

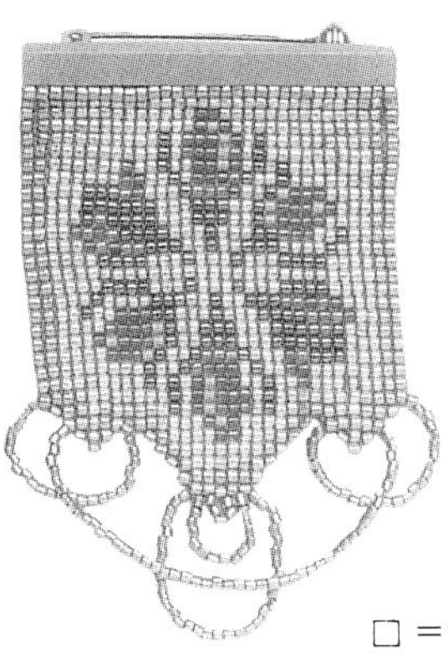

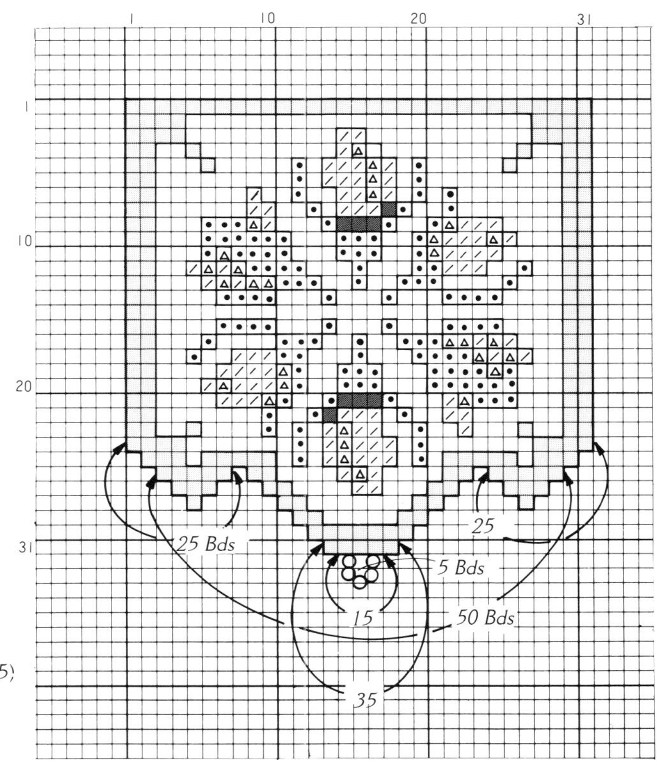

□ = Silver (TB558)
□ = Gold (TB712)
■ = Yellow Green (TB775)
◙ = Green (TB507)
◪ = Red (TB241)
◬ = Pink (TB145)

Tulip Brooch & Earring

Pictured on page 8

● MATERIALS

Beads . . Red 2g, Yellow Green 1g, Green 1g, Dark Green 1g, Gold 1g, Silver1g
Thread . . . . .Gray
Supplies . . Brooch Helmet Shaped Pin, Gold Earring Findings
Horizontal x Vertical rows: Brooch . . . . .9 x 32
Horizontal x Vertical rows: Earing . . . . .9 x 11
Number of Warp Threads 10

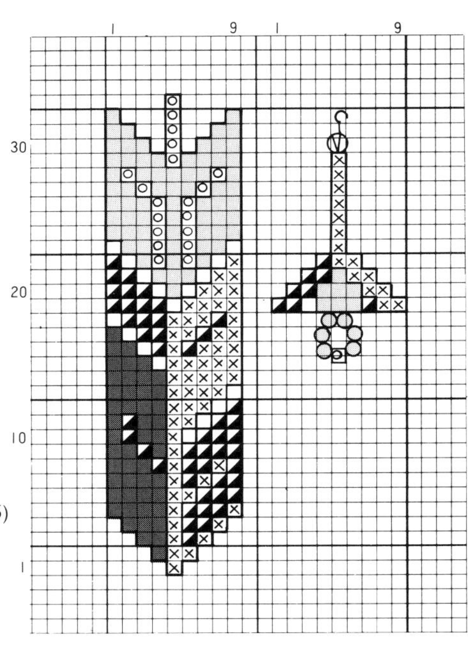

☐ = Red (TB241)
◪ = Yellow Green (TB775)
☒ = Green (TB507)
■ = Dark Green (TB508)
☐ = Silver (TB21)
⊡ = Gold (TB22)

Lily Pendant

Pictured on page 8

● MATERIALS

Beads . . . . .Frosted Black 3g
Frosted Green 2g, Silver 1g
Thread . . . . .Black
Horizontal x Vertical rows . . . . .21 x 28
Number of Warp Threads 22

With frosted black and green beads, the pendant will gain calm. The string is fitted at the center of the beaded panel for stability.

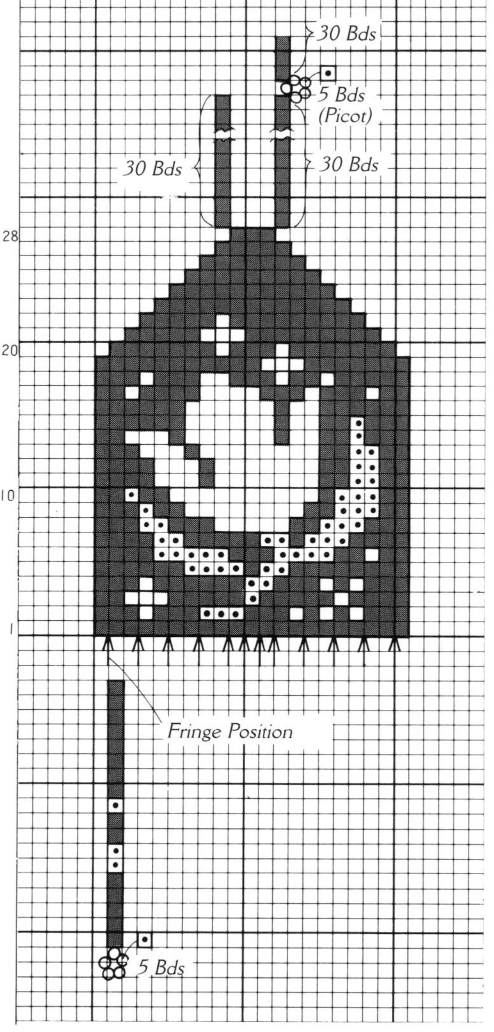

■ = Frosted Black (TB610)
⊡ = Frosted Green (TB710)
☐ = Silver (TB558)

Leaf Pendant

Pictured on page 10

● MATERIALS

Beads . . Purple 4g, Light Purple 5g, Nickel 4g
Thread . . . . .Gray
Supplies . . . . .Chain Set, Silver
Horizontal x Vertical rows .15 x 30
Number of Warp Threads 16

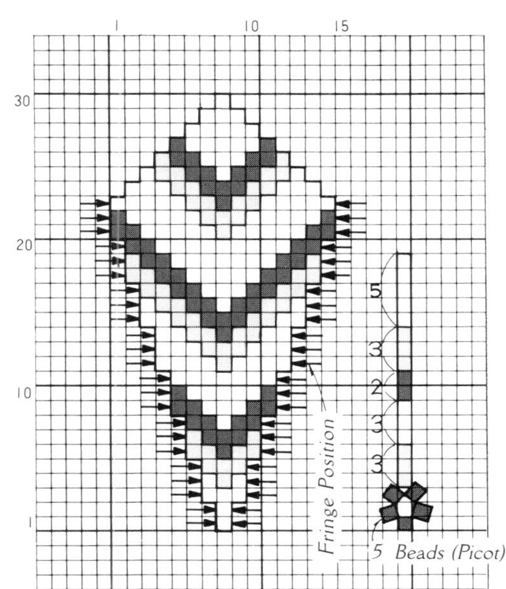

☐ = Light Purple (TB425)
■ = Nickel (TB711)
☐ = Purple (TB504)

Heart Brooch & Earring

Pictured on page 8

● MATERIALS

Beads . . . . Black 4g, Light Blue 2g
Thread . . . . .Black
Supplies . . . . .Brooch Helmet Shaped Pin, Gold Earring Findings
Horizontal x Vertical rows, Brooch . . . . .19 x 19
Horizontal x Vertical rows, Brooch . . . . .13 x 13
Horizontal x Vertical rows, Earring . . . . .11 x 11
Number of Threads, Brooch 20, 14
Number of Threads, Earring 12

Brooch is made by weaving large and small panels and attaching fringes. Finish the work by fitting ball tip at the top of panel, and put fringes through panel in direction of arrows.

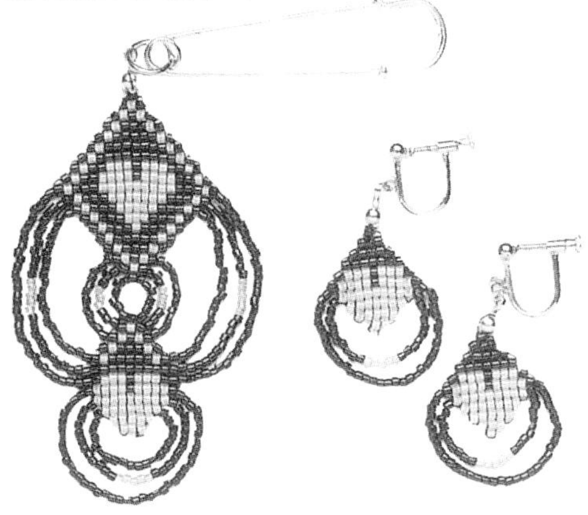

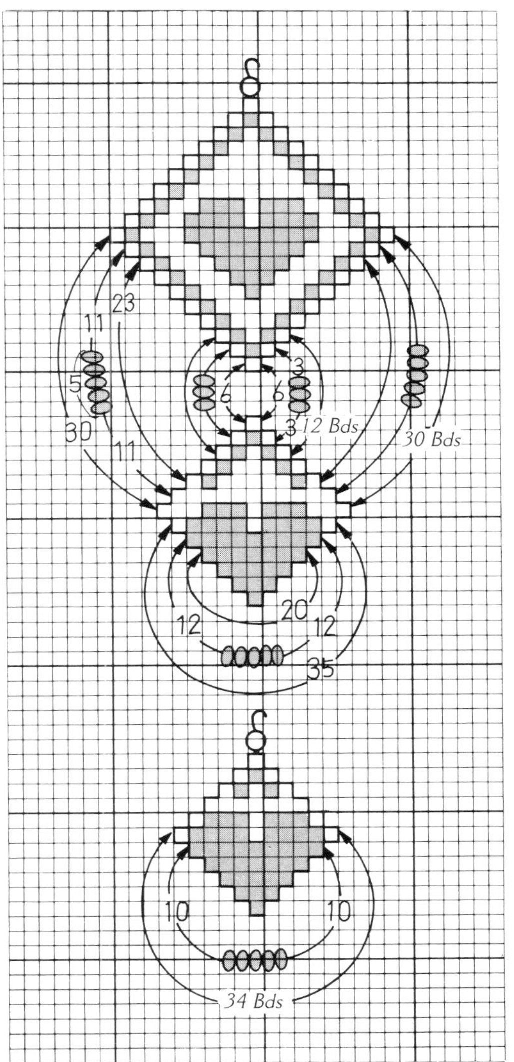

☐ = Black (TB49)
☐ = Light Blue (TB787)

Secret Box Pendant

Pictured on page 11

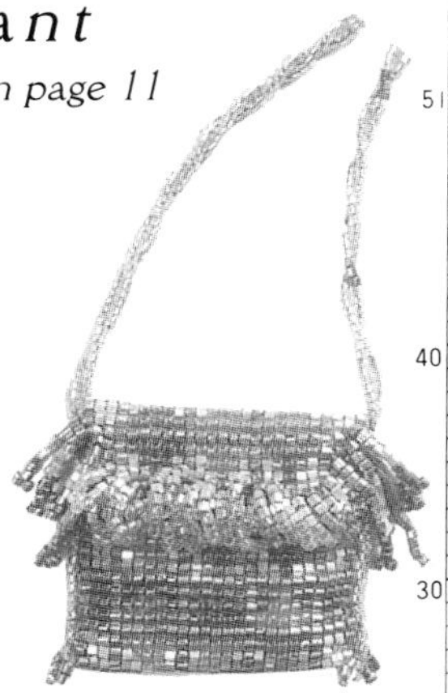

MATERIALS

Beads . . . . . . Pink 1g, Light Blue 1g, ...Bluish Purple 1g, Nickel 3g, ...Silver 4g, Gold 5g
Thread . . . . .Gray
Supplies . . . . .Chain Set, Silver
Horizontal x Vertical rows . .25 x 51
Number of Warp Threads 26

Finish working panel and stitch the side, A and B, forming it into bag. The cover section is fitted with looped fringe and the rope handle is made by putting two lines of thread through beads and stitching on the side. Mix Pink, Light Blue and Bluish Purple beads.

mix ■ = Pink (TB909)
= Light Blue (TB328)
= Bluish Purple (TB788)
□ = Nickel (TB711)
⊙ = Silver (TB558)
⊠ = Gold (TB712)

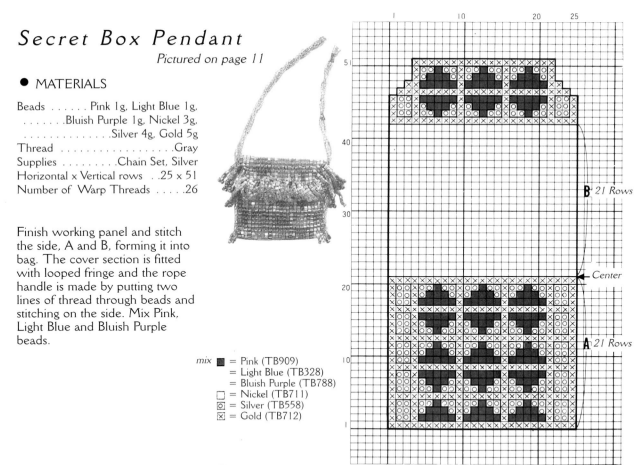

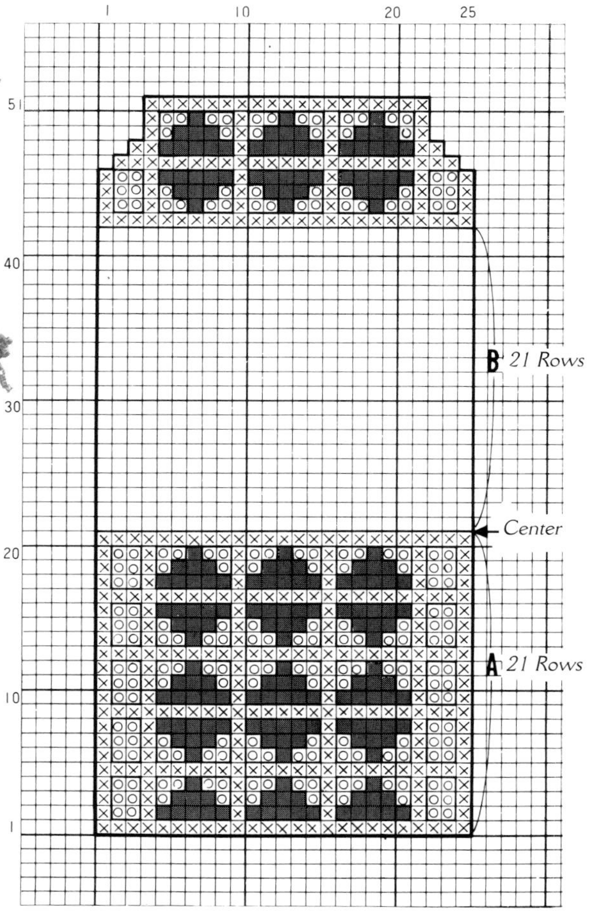

B 21 Rows
Center
A 21 Rows

Echo Pendant & Earring

Pictured on page 8

MATERIALS

Beads . . . . Gold 2g, Frosted Blue 2g
Green 2g, Frosted Green 2g
Thread . . . . .Gray
Supplies . . . . .Chain Set,
Gold Earring Finding
Horizontal x Vertical rows
Pendant . . . . .21 x 29
Earring . . . . .7 x 19
Number of Warp Threads
Pendant 22

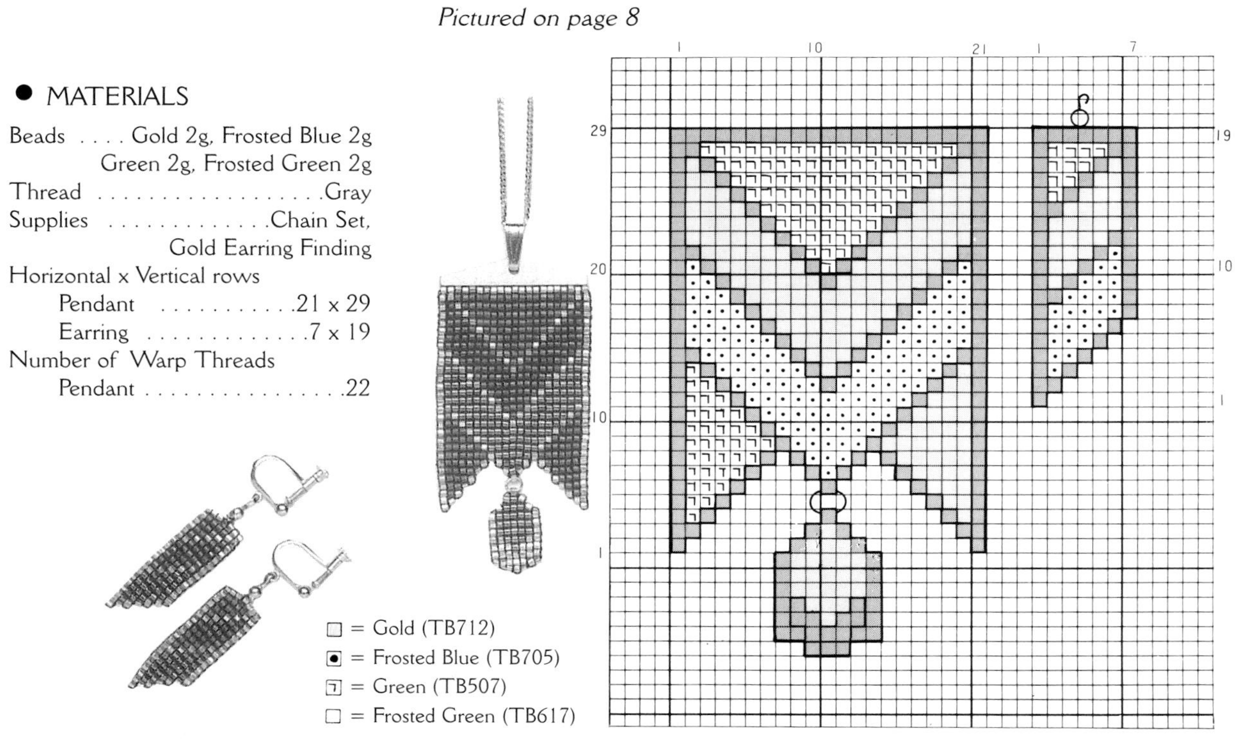

Christmas Tree Pendant

Pictured on page 8

- MATERIALS

Beads . . Silver 5g, Green 1g, Gold 1g, Dark Gold 1g, Purplish Red 20 bds, Charcoal 20 bds, Light Blue 20 bds, Red 30 bds.
Thread . . . . Gray
Horizontal x Vertical rows . . . . 21 x 27
Number of Warp Threads 22

□ = Silver (TB558)
□ = Green (TB507)
⊠ = Red (TB25)
⊡ = Dark Gold (TB221)
■ = Gold (TB712)
▲ = Purplish Red (TB785)
◎ = Light Blue (TB23)
▨ = Charcoal (TB81)

Fringe position
15 Beads
5 Beads
15, 13, 10, 10, 13, 15, 13, 10, 10, 13

White House Pendant & Earring

Pictured on page 9

- MATERIALS

Beads . . . . Dark Gold 4g, Other colors 1g each
Thread . . . . Gray
Supplies . . . . Silver Earring Findings
Horizontal x Vertical rows: Pendant . . . . 21 x 28
Horizontal x Vertical rows: Earring . . . . 9 x 10
Number of Warp Threads . . 22 Pendant, 10 Earring

8 Bds
2 Bds
1 Bds
2 Bds
5 Bds
Ring 5 Bds

■ = Dark Gold (TB221)
⊡ = Dark Blue (TB82)
△ = Violet (TB771)
⊠ = Iridescence (TB509)
⊡ = Light Blue (TB792)
□ = Silver (TB558)
▨ = Blue (TB776)
□ = Green (TB507)
◎ = Red Gold (TB502)
▦ = Frosted Blue (TB612)
◪ = Gold (TB712)
☑ = Dark Green (TB508)

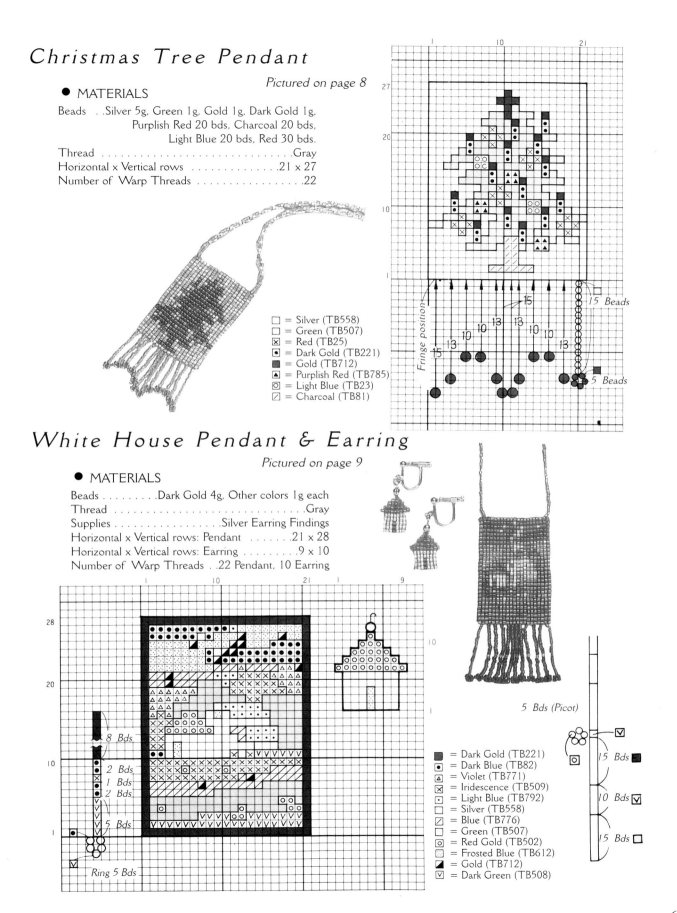

5 Bds (Picot)
15 Bds
10 Bds
15 Bds

Slit Necklace & Earring

Pictured on page 10

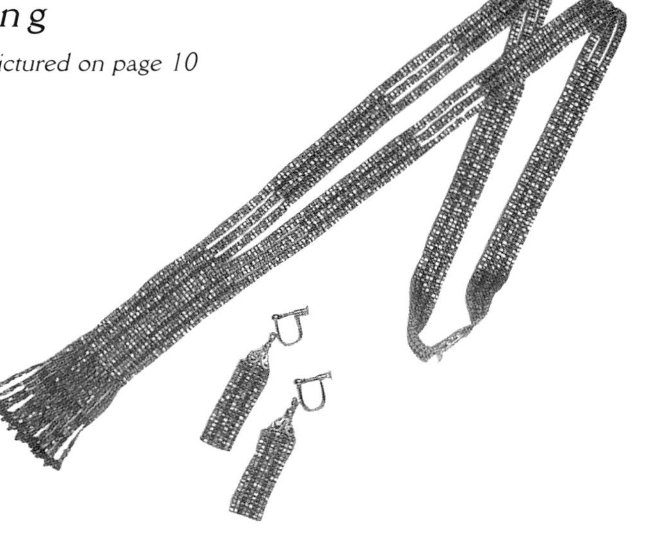

● MATERIALS

Beads .Purple 4g, Nickel 23g
Thread . . . . .Gray
Supplies . . . . . .Silver Necklace and Earring Findings
Horizontal x Vertical rows:Necklace . . . . . .16 x 244
Horizontal x Vertical rows:Earring . . . . .8 x 11
Number of Warp Threads: Necklace . .18 x 90 cm
Earrings 9

NECKLACE

1. Weave center section, every other warp thread doubled after 2nd bead. Separate warps into two for right and left sides, 9 on each side. See page 53.

2. Weave sections of band: 2 stitch bands x 22 rows and 8 stitch bands x 34 rows.

3. Go on weaving according to the pattern, finish and fit findings.

EARRING

1. Weave 21 rows, and reduce weaving stitches one by one on both ends.

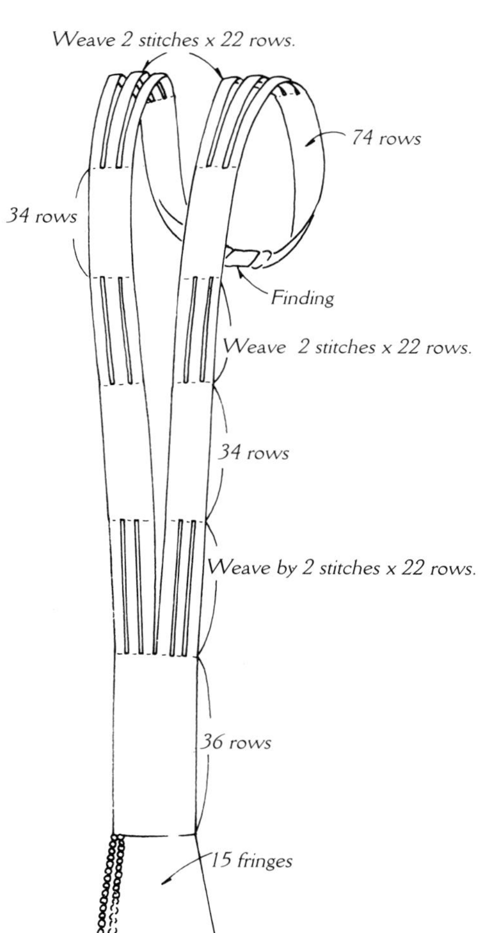

▣ = Purple (TB85)
□ = Nickel (TB711)

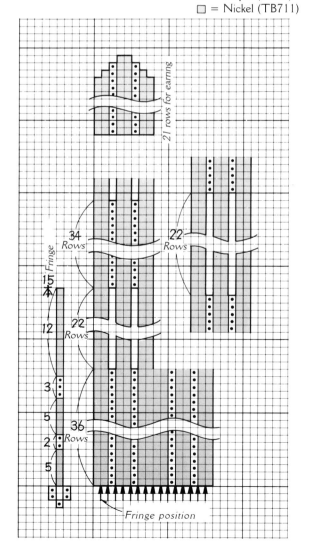

21 rows for earring
34 Rows
22 Rows
Fringe 15 本
12
22 Rows
3
5
36 Rows
2
5
Fringe position

Three Braid Necklace & Earring

Pictured on page 10

- MATERIALS

Beads . . . . .Black 24g, Nickel 5g, Purple 4g
Thread . . . . .Black
Supplies .Silver Earring Set
Horizontal x Vertical rows:Necklace . . . . . .16 x 270
Horizontal x Vertical rows:Earring . . . . .13 x 20
Number of Warp Threads: Necklace . .18 x 90 cm
Earring .14

NECKLACE

1. Weave pendant section, doubling warp threads between every other bead after second bead. Weave right and left bands to 30 rows. See general instructions, page 53.
2. Weave three bands 2 beads wide on right and left sides to 30 rows and braid those three bands. Continue to 160 rows, following diagram and join right and left bands.
3. Attach 15 fringe strands to pendant.

EARRINGS

Attach fringes and findings to panel.

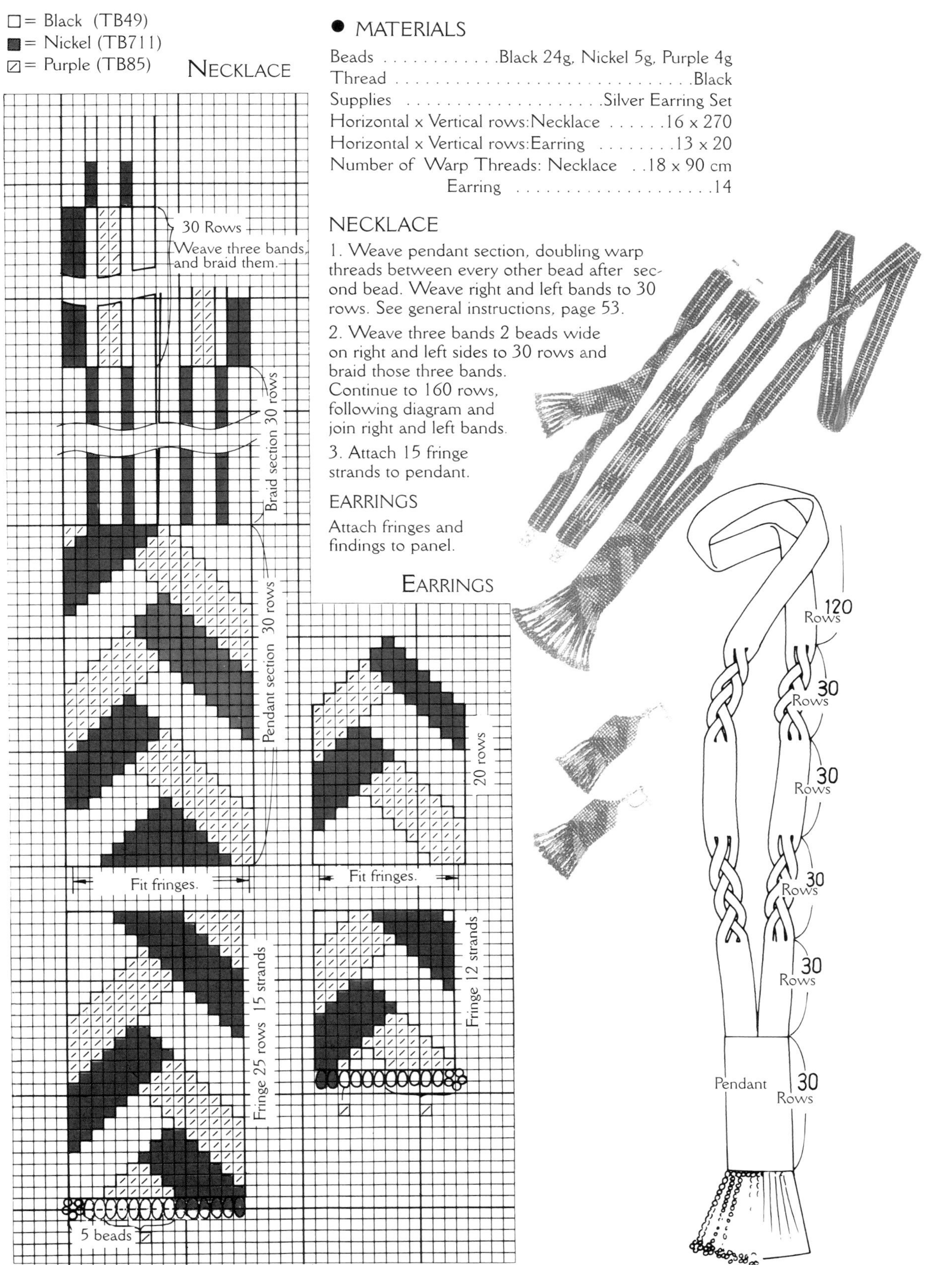

Evening Collar *Pictured on page 5*

● MATERIALS

Beads . . . . .Silver (TB21) 25g
Thread . . . . .Beige
Supplies . . . . .Silver Clasp
Number of Warp Threads 29

● TECHNIQUE

1. Weave a band 7 beads wide x 130 rows.
2. Weave 4 triangular motifs, and stitch them together. Join to band, centering on band.
3. For triangular motifs, start with 17 beads and reduce one stitch on both sides every 3 rows, continuing to weave to 27th row. See page 46 for terminating warp threads.
4. Put beads in the A, B and C spaces, tieing them to each other. Fit clasp to band. See page 48 for "Pineap- "Pineapple" fringe.

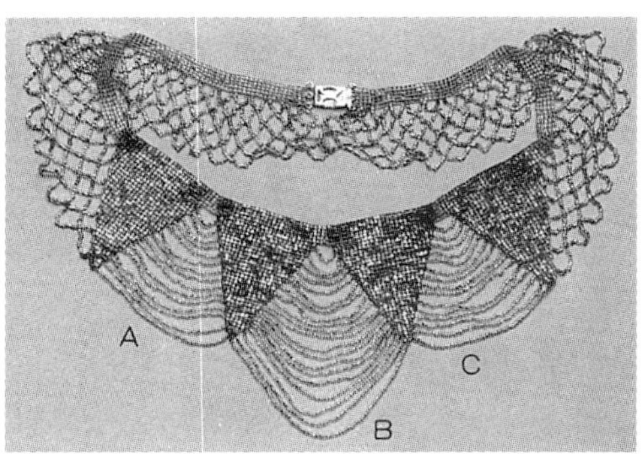

FITTING CLASP

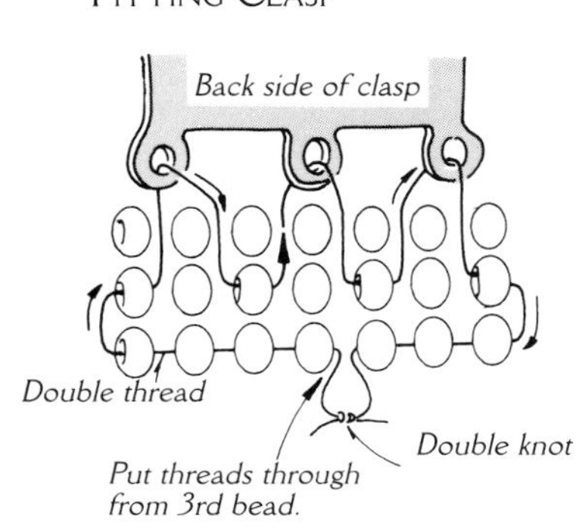

SCENT BAG PENDANT

pictured on page 10

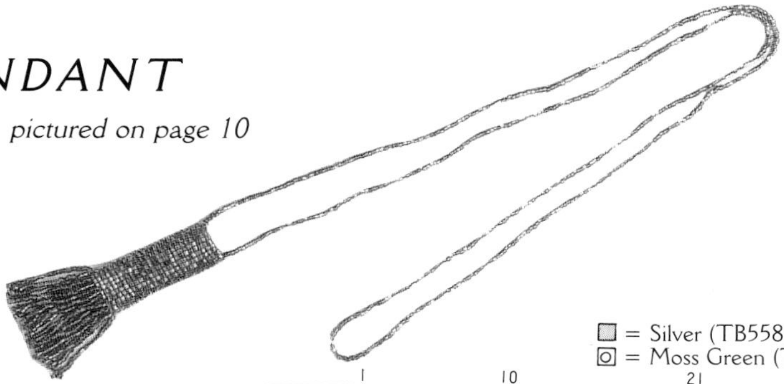

● MATERIALS

Beads . . . . .Silver 5g, Moss Green 3g
Thread . . . . .Gray
Horizontal x Vertical rows . . .21 x 24
Number of Warp Threads 22

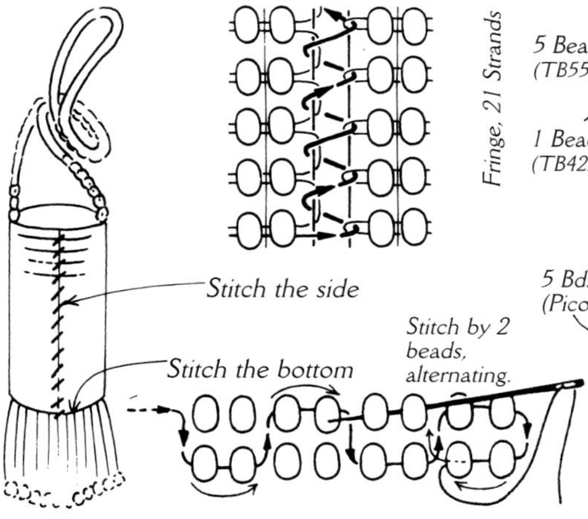

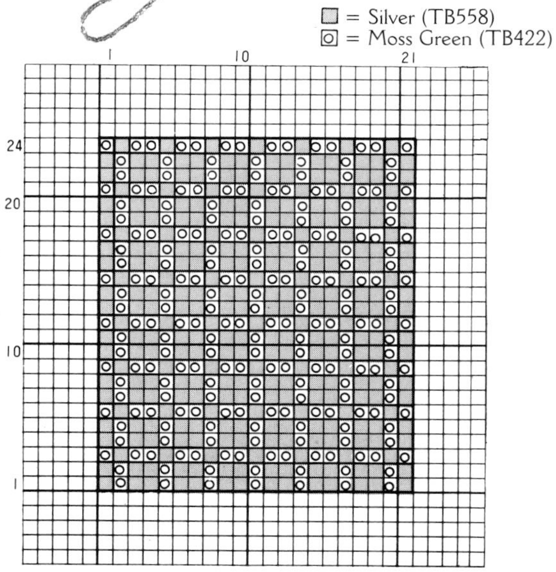

Stitch the side
Stitch the bottom
Stitch by 2 beads, alternating.

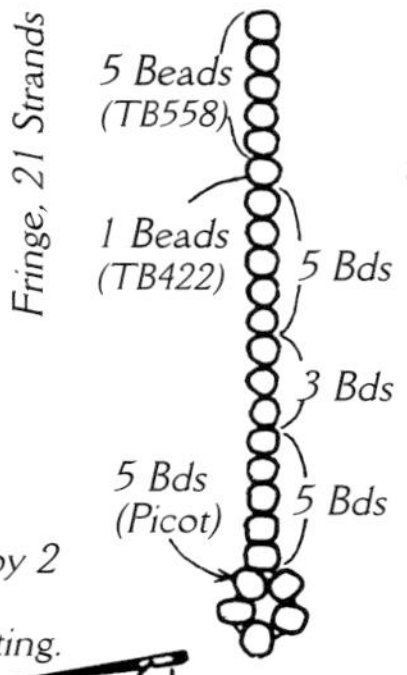

Fringe, 21 Strands
5 Beads (TB558)
1 Beads (TB422)
5 Bds
3 Bds
5 Bds (Picot)
5 Bds

▢ = Silver (TB558)
◙ = Moss Green (TB422)

Crystal Collar

Pictured on page 3

● MATERIALS

Beads ...... Silver (TB558) 40g, Silver (TB21) 40g
Thread .... Beige
Horizontal x Vertical Rows .... 25 x 40
Number of Warp Threads 26

25 Beads
PANEL: 12 Required
33 Rows
25th Stitch
19
13
9
7
5
3
1st Stitch

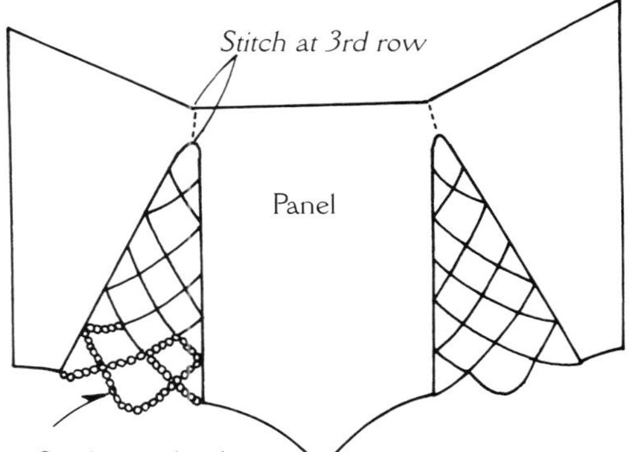

Winter Corsage

Pictured on page 6

● MATERIALS

Beads . Gold (TB712) 10g, Dark Gold (TB221) 10g,
Red Gold (TB222) 10g, Iridescence (TB509) 12g,
Green (TB507) 6g
Thread .... Gray
Supplies .... #28 Gold Wire, 30cm x 14

● TECHNIQUE

1. Make 4 large petals, 3 medium petals, 3 small petals and 3 leaves.
2. Put wire through base of petals, apply glue and make a cupped form after drying.
3. Mesh 2 small petals, and place remaining small petal, medium petals and large petals in order, and then fit the 3 leaves underneath.
4. Put them together in corsage for completion.

PETAL AND LEAF ACTUAL SIZE

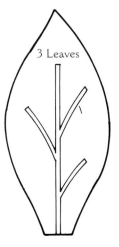

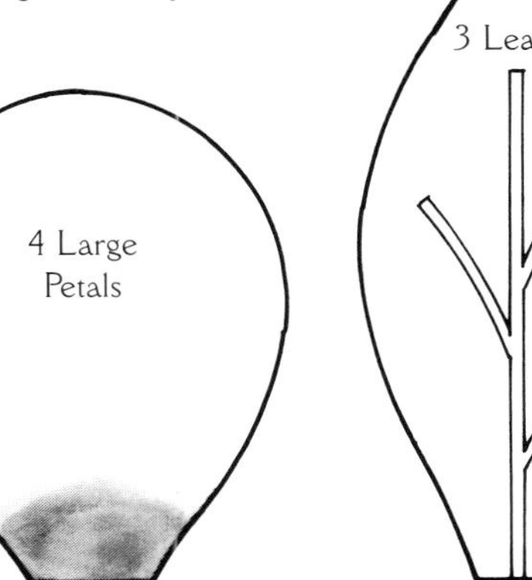

Sash Bands

Pictured on page 17

● MATERIALS

Beads . . . . .Purple 65g, Silver 20g, Gold 4g
Thread . . . . .Gray
Horizontal & Vertical Rows . . . .15 x approx 150cm
Number of Warp Threads . . . . .32 x 180 cm
Fringe . . . . .16 Strands

● TECHNIQUE

1. Prepare 16 double warp threads.
2. Weave about 150cm long according to the size of waist.

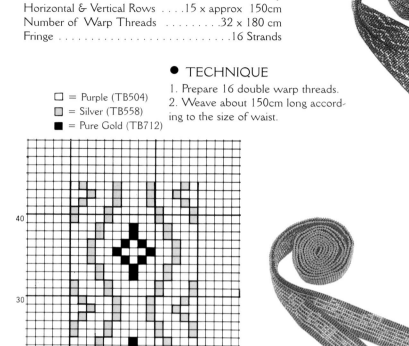

□ = Purple (TB504)
▩ = Silver (TB558)
■ = Pure Gold (TB712)

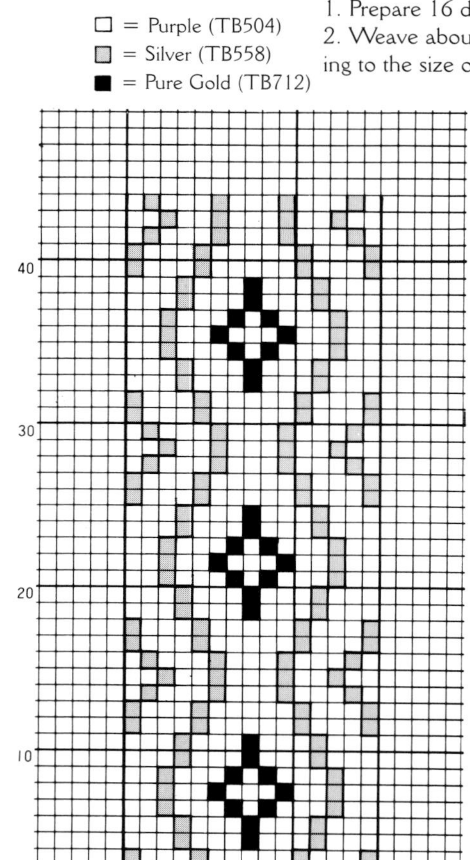

Frame

Melody

Woven 2cm wide and about 150cm long. Cross it at the chest for a necklace or use it like belt. The pattern is like the notes of a song.

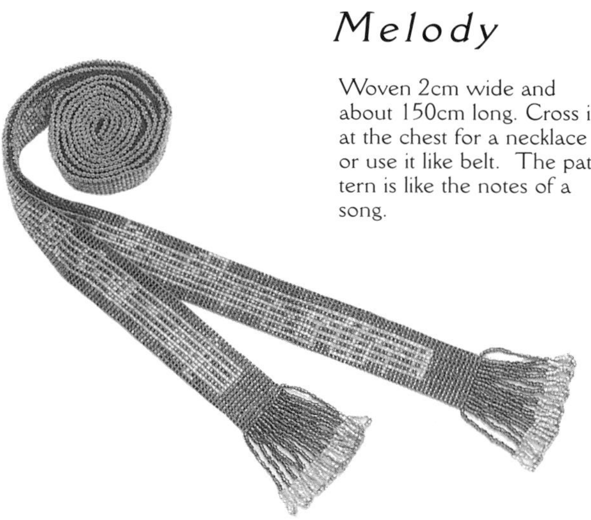

Ripples

This band is designed in the image of ripples with the graduation of various colors.

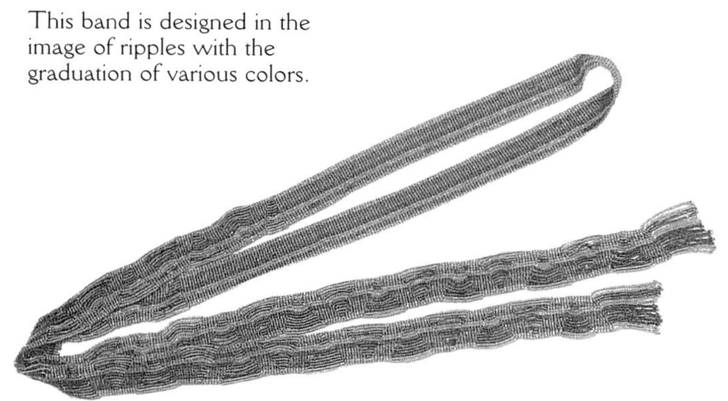

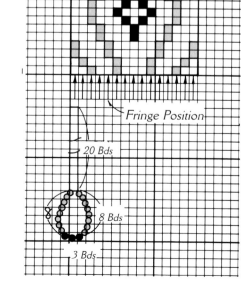

Spring Breeze Necktie

Pictured on page 12

- MATERIALS

Beads . . . . .Listed Below
Thread . . . . .Gray
Horizontal & Vertical Rows . . . . .29 x 684
Warp Threads .140cm x 30

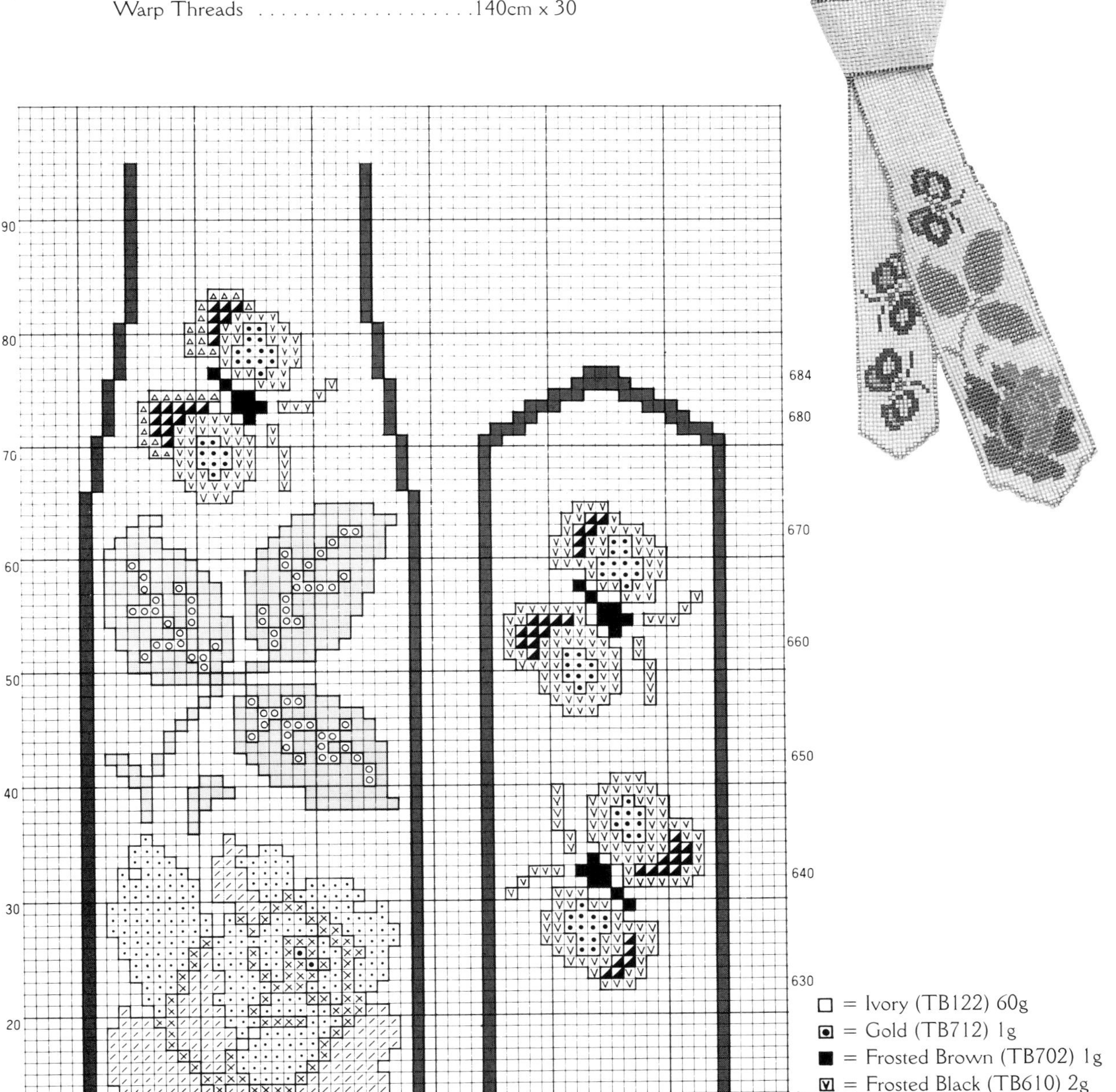

□ = Ivory (TB122) 60g
⊡ = Gold (TB712) 1g
■ = Frosted Brown (TB702) 1g
V = Frosted Black (TB610) 2g
△ = Black (TB49) 1g
◪ = Blue (TB776) 1g
□ = Green (TB507) 1g
○ = Dark Gold (TB221) 1g
⊡ = Red (TB241) 2g
⧄ = Wine Red (TB332) 1g
⊠ = Violet (TB771) 1g
■ = Nickel (TB711) 8g

Roses In May Eyeglass Case

Pictured on page 12

● MATERIALS

Beads .... Listed Below
Thread .... Black
Supplies .... Gold Snap
Lining, Black Satin 40cm x 13cm
Horizontal & Vertical Rows .... 62 x 105
Warp .... 90cm x 63

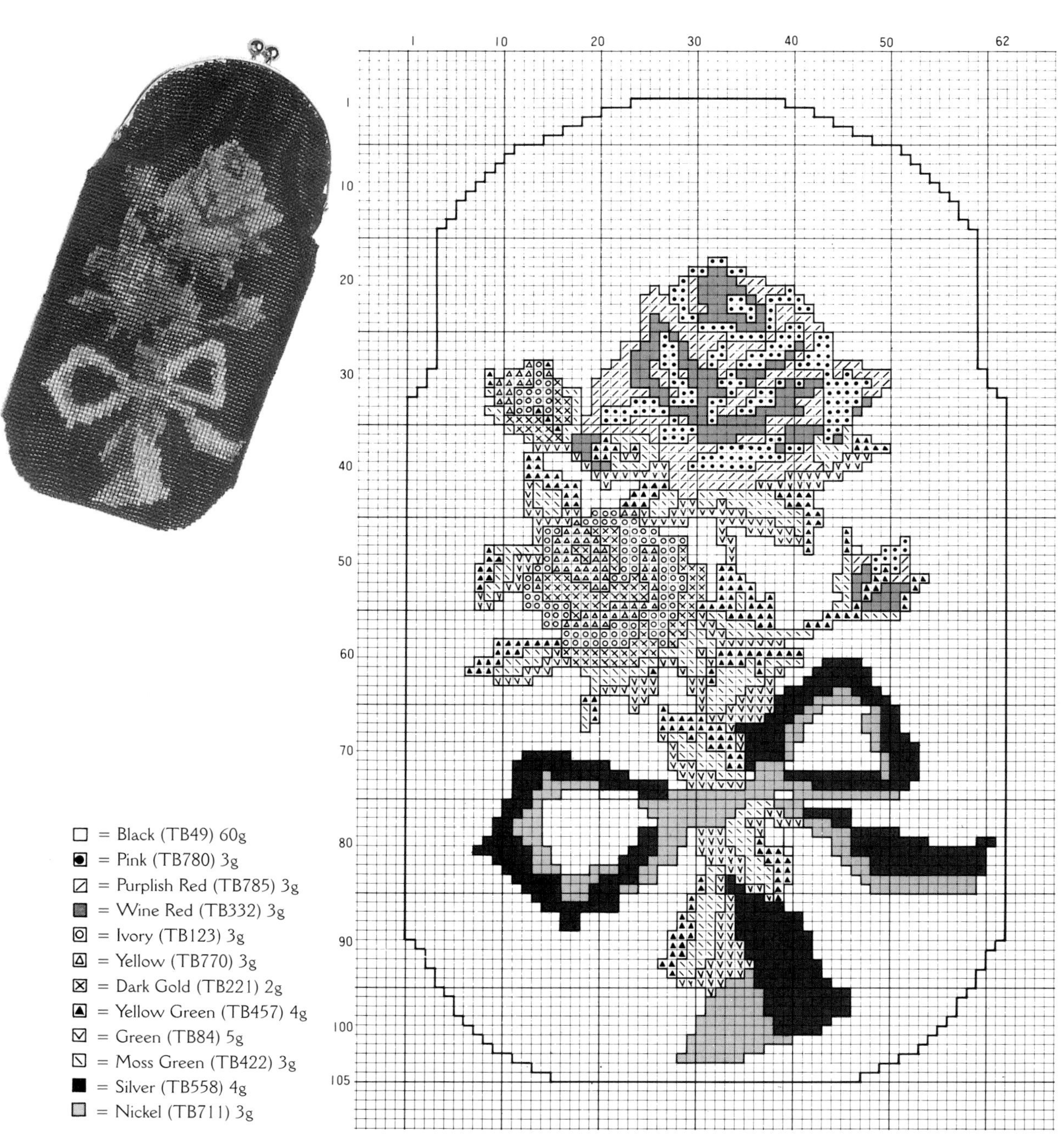

- ☐ = Black (TB49) 60g
- ◙ = Pink (TB780) 3g
- ⧄ = Purplish Red (TB785) 3g
- ▩ = Wine Red (TB332) 3g
- ⊡ = Ivory (TB123) 3g
- ⚠ = Yellow (TB770) 3g
- ☒ = Dark Gold (TB221) 2g
- ▲ = Yellow Green (TB457) 4g
- ☑ = Green (TB84) 5g
- ⧅ = Moss Green (TB422) 3g
- ■ = Silver (TB558) 4g
- ▢ = Nickel (TB711) 3g

Rose Arch Eyeglass Case

Pictured on page 12

● MATERIALS

Beads . . . . Listed Below
Thread . . . . Gray
Supplies . . . . Gold Snap
Lining, White Satin 40cm x 13cm
Horizontal & Vertical Rows . . . . 62 x 106
Warp . . . . 90cm x 63

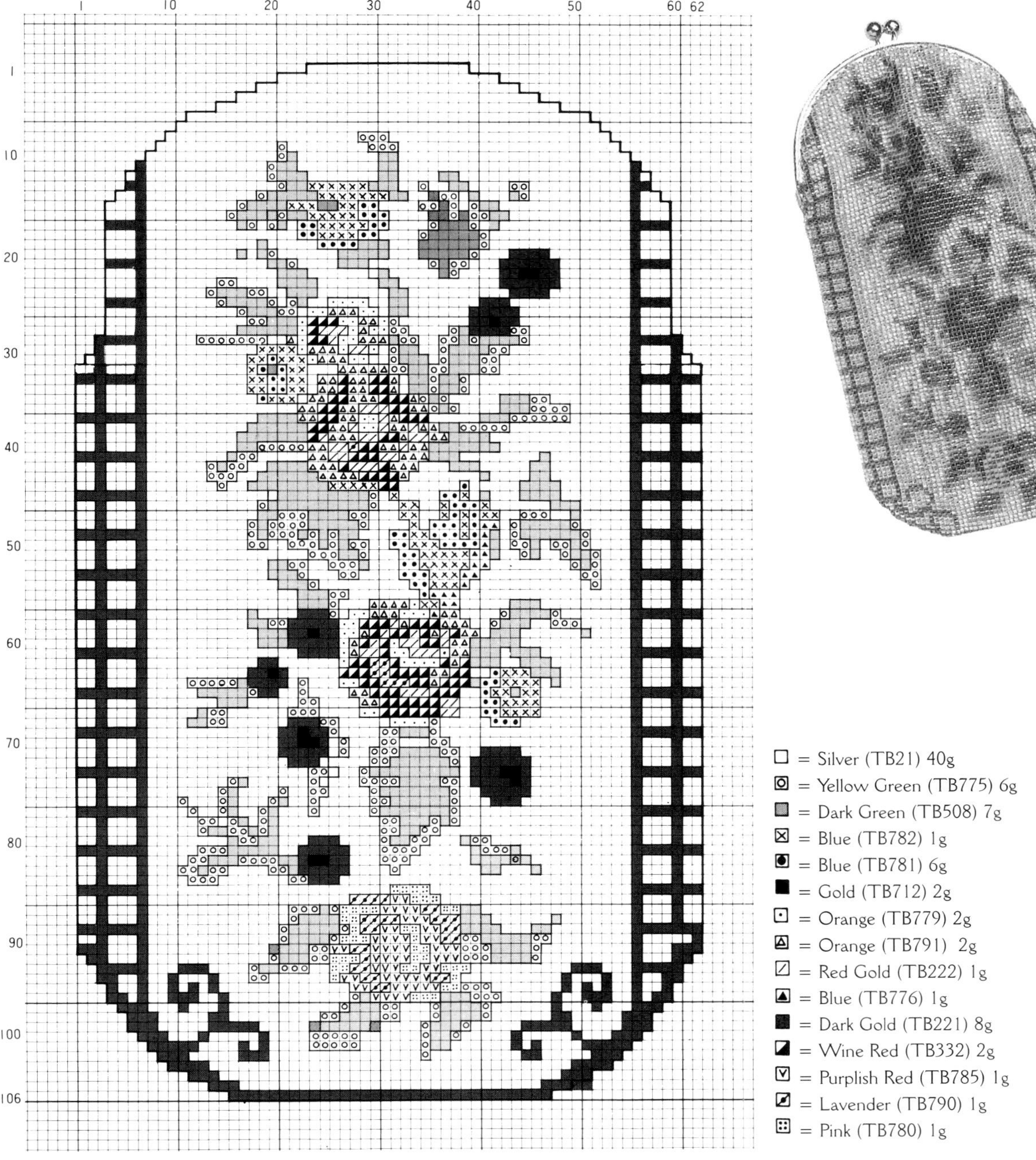

□ = Silver (TB21) 40g
▣ = Yellow Green (TB775) 6g
▩ = Dark Green (TB508) 7g
☒ = Blue (TB782) 1g
◙ = Blue (TB781) 6g
■ = Gold (TB712) 2g
⊡ = Orange (TB779) 2g
◬ = Orange (TB791) 2g
◱ = Red Gold (TB222) 1g
▲ = Blue (TB776) 1g
■ = Dark Gold (TB221) 8g
◪ = Wine Red (TB332) 2g
🅅 = Purplish Red (TB785) 1g
◩ = Lavender (TB790) 1g
⚃ = Pink (TB780) 1g

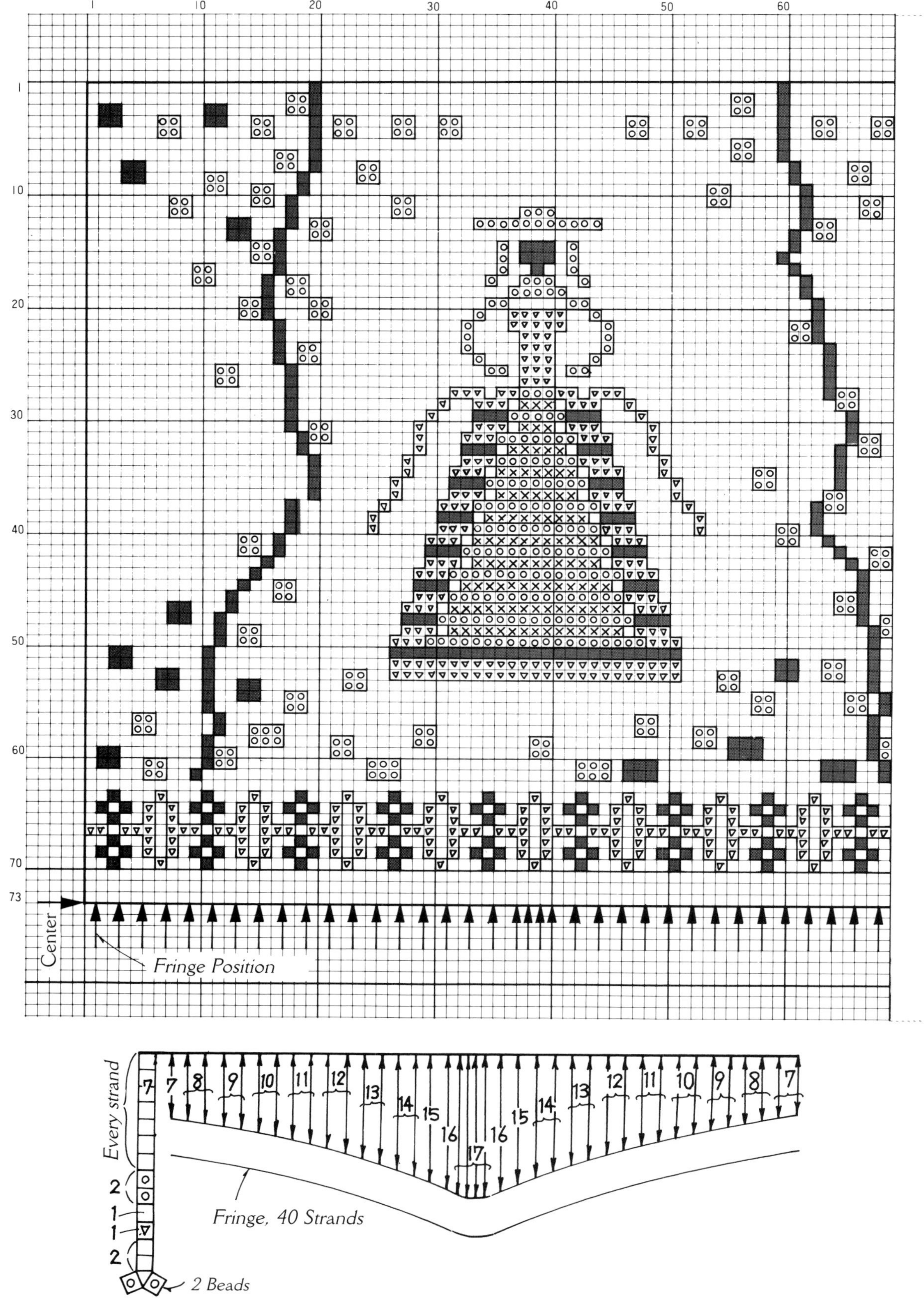
Center
Fringe Position
Every strand
Fringe, 40 Strands
2 Beads

70 77

BAND

Promenade Pouch

Pictured on page 12

● MATERIALS

Beads . . . . Listed Below
Thread . . . . Black
Supplies . . . . Black closure
Lining, Black Satin 30cm x 50cm
Horizontal & Vertical Rows: Bag . . . . 77 x 73
Horizontal & Vertical Rows: Strap . . . . 7 x 72
Warp . . . . 90cm x 78
Fringe . . . . 40 Strands

● TECHNIQUE

1. Warp 78 threads, 90cm long.
2. Weave from 1st row to 73th row according to pattern, and return to the 1st row.
3. Sew inner bag and attach closure and decorative band.

☐ = Black (TB49) 50g
■ = Dark Gold (TB221) 4g
⊡ = Gold (TB712) 6g
⊽ = Red Gold (TB222) 5g
⊠ = Mixed (TB-507,780,790,775,792,782,332) 5g

Graceful Bag

Pictured on page 5

● MATERIALS

Beads . .Silver (TB558) 50g, Iridescence (TB721) 160g
Thread . . . . .Gray
Supplies . . . . .Lining, White Satin 30cm x 40cm
Horizontal & Vertical Rows: Bag . . . . .140 x 100
Horizontal & Vertical Rows: Strap . . . . .6 x 312
Warp . . . . .90cm x 141

● TECHNIQUE

1. Warp 141 threads, 90cm long.
2. Weave the left pattern symmetrically.
3. Attach fringes at the opening .
4. Weave strap 1 silver, 4 iridescence, 1 silver, each row
5. Attach strap after weaving 312 rows.

Draw String Bag

Pictured on page 4

Curve the hem in 3 rows to vary the form, the pattern being very simple. Beads are nickel (TB721). Seven accent colors are used, and the work is finished in pure silver metallic.

Put 2 strands of decorative cord through slits and terminate with lovely paper lanterns (see page 109). Inspiration is from Broadway stage play "My Fair Lady."

■ = Silver (TB558)
□ = Iridescence (TB721)
1
10
20
30
40
50
60
70
Center
1
10
20
30
40
50
60
70
80
90
100
Center

Radish Brooch & Earring

pictured on page 8

● MATERIALS

Beads . . . . .Listed below
Thread . . . . .Gray
Supplies . . . . .Brooch pin, Gold earring set
Horizontal & Vertical Rows: Brooch . . . . . . .12 x 20
Horizontal & Vertical Rows: Earring . . . . .9 x 8
Warp . . . . .Brooch: 21; Earring: 9

□ = Silver (TB558) 1g
⊡ = Green (TB507) 1g
L = Yellow Green (TB775) 1g
■ = Wine Red (TB332) 2g
△ = Violet (TB771) 1g
V = Nickel (TB711) 1g
⧅ = Dark Green (TB508)1g
● = Pink (TB780) 1g
⊥ = Moss Green (TB422) 1g

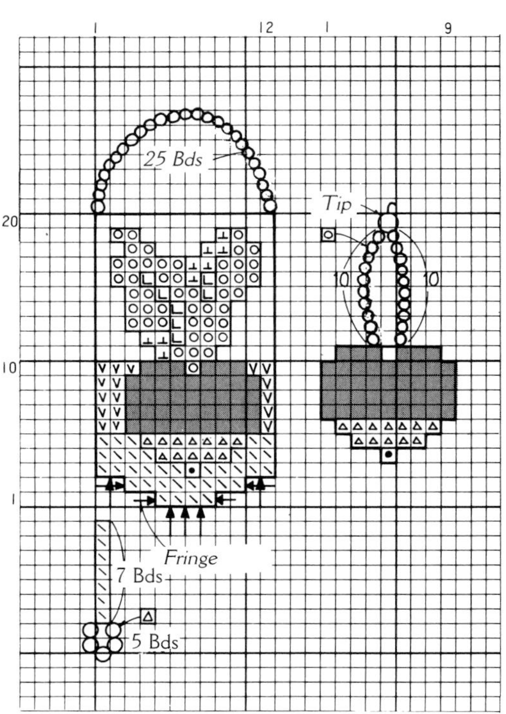

Parisienne" Bag

Pictured on page 7

● MATERIALS

Beads . . . . .Dark Gold 100g, Dark Brown 80g
Thread . . . . .Gray
Supplies . . . . .Lining, White Satin 30cm x 40cm
Horizontal & Vertical Rows: Bag . . . . .121 x 108
Horizontal & Vertical Rows: Strap . . . . .5 x 312
Warp . . . . .90cm x 122
Fringe . . . . .33 Beads x 60 strands

● TECHNIQUE

1. Warp 122 threads 90cm long.
2. Make slits from 7th row.
3. Weave strap. 3 Dark Gold, 2 Dark Brown x 312 rows.
4. Put strap through slits and knot it.
5. Sew lining cloth to beads of 2nd row from the lower side of slit.

■ = Dark Gold (TB221)
☒ = Dark Brown (TB83)

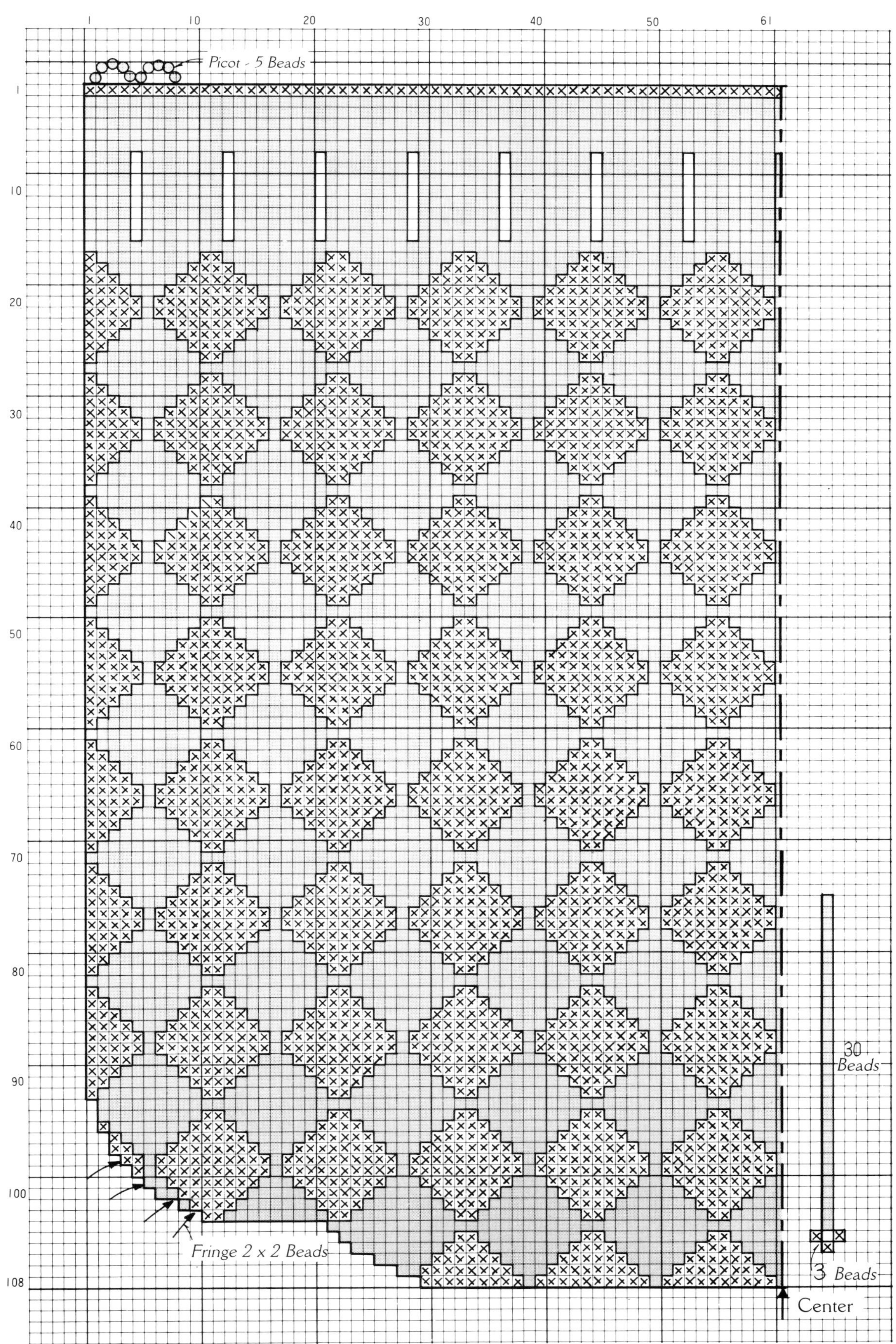
Picot - 5 Beads
Fringe 2 x 2 Beads
30 Beads
3 Beads
Center
1
10
20
30
40
50
61
1
10
20
30
40
50
60
70
80
90
100
108

Reticule (Money Pouch)

Pictured on cover

● MATERIALS

Beads . . . . .Listed Below
Thread . . . . .Gray
Supplies . . . . .Lining, White Satin 50cm x 50cm
Horizontal & Vertical Rows . . . . .42 x 110
Warp . . . . .90cm x 43

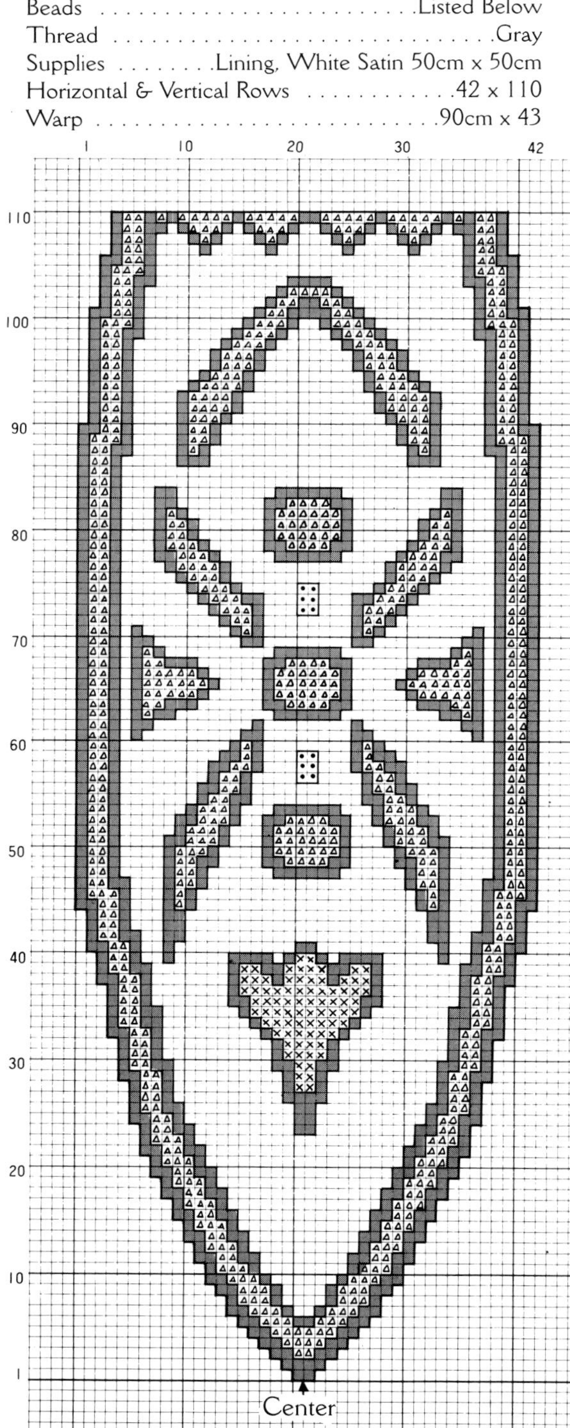

● TECHNIQUE

1. Weave 6 panels, 42 stitches x 110 rows each.
2. Sew panels together at the sides to make it a sphere shape.
3. Fit inner bag and also sew it after putting through tying string.
4. Weave strap 8 beads wide by a length for wearing.
5. For accessories worn about the neck, shape bag by putting cotton inside.
6. Make 10 fringes by stringing beads in 20cm lengths. Make into a tassel by making strands into loops and then tying them in a circle.

□ = Silver (TB558) 80g
⊿ = Gold (TB712) 60g
■ = Nickel (TB711) 40g
⊙ = Green (TB507) 2g
⊠ = Pink (TB780) 3g

Party Brooch

Pictured on page 9

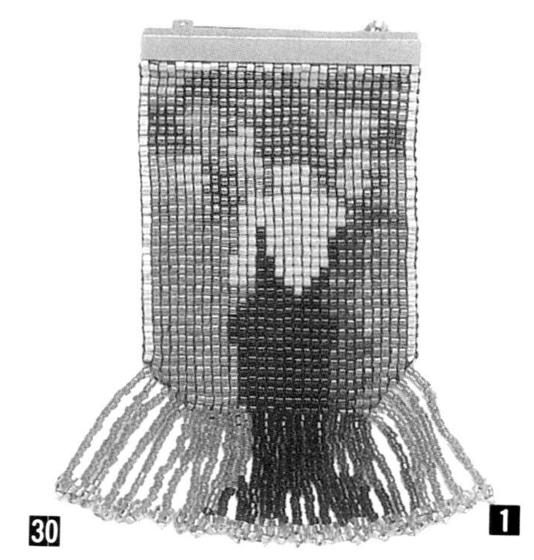

● MATERIALS

Beads . . . . .Listed Below
Thread . . . . .Gray
Supplies . . . . .Gold Bar
Horizontal & Vertical Rows . . . . .31 x 36
Warp Threads 32

Row																
1	31															
2	1	5×	2♯	2×	4◐	1×	1♯	3×	2♯	4×	5⊙	1				
3	1	3×	4♯	3×	2◐	13×	4⊙	1								
4	1	3×	10♯	1▲	3○	9×	3⊙	1								
5	1	9×	3♯	4▲	2○	1♯	3×	2●	2×	3♯	1					
6	1	2♯	2×	3◎	1×	3♯	5▲	2♯	3×	4●	4×	1				
7	1	3×	4◎	3♯	7▲	1×	4♯	4●	3×	1						
8	1	4×	2◎	3♯	8▲	2◐	2×	2♯	2●	4×	1					
9	1	7×	2♯	8▲	4◐	3♯	5×	1								
10	1	4×	2⊙	2×	1♯	8▲	3◐	1×	2♯	6×	1					
11	1	4♯	3⊙	3×	6▲	3◐	2♯	2×	2◎	4♯	1					
12	1	2♯	3×	3⊙	3×	4△	1♯	2◐	1♯	4×	3◎	3♯	1			
13	1	2♯	2×	4⊙	2×	1♯	4△	1×	3♯	3×	4◎	3♯	1			
14	1	3♯	2×	2⊙	2×	2♯	4○	1×	4♯	3×	2◎	4♯	1			
15	1	2♯	2▫	4×	10△	4×	1▫	2♯	1▫	1⧈	2▫	1				
16	1	2⧈	4◘	1⧈	12△	3×	2⧈	2♯	3⧈	1						
17	1	7◘	12△	2⧈	2×	2⧈	1♯	3⧈	1							
18	1	2⧈	1▫	1⧈	3◘	1■	8△	1■	2△	2⧈	1▫	2⧈	2▫	3⧈	1	
19	1	2⧈	1▫	2⧈	3◘	1■	7△	1■	2△	3⧈	1▫	2⧈	4▫	1		
20	1	3⧈	1◘	1▫	3◘	1■	7△	1■	2△	1×	3⧈	1▫	3⧈	2▫	1	
21	1	3⧈	1▫	4◘	1■	6△	2■	3△	1▫	2⧈	1▫	2⧈	3▫	1		
22	1	5⧈	4◘	1■	5△	2■	3△	3⧈	1▫	3⧈	2▫	1				
23	1	3⧈	1◘	3⧈	2◘	2■	3△	3■	1⧈	2△	4⧈	1▫	1⧈	3▫	1	
24	1	4⧈	2▫	4◘	2■	1△	4■	1⧈	1▫	2⧈	1▫	3⧈	1▫	3⧈	1	
25	1	4⧈	1▫	2⧈	3◘	8■	2⧈	1▫	3⧈	1▫	1⧈	3▫	1			
26	1	5⧈	4◘	10■	3⧈	1▫	3⧈	3▫	1							
27	1	5⧈	3◘	12■	4⧈	2▫	3⧈	1								
28	1	2▫	3⧈	3◘	12■	2⧈	3▫	4⧈	1							
29	1	4⧈	4◘	12■	3⧈	1▫	2⧈	3▫	1							
30	1	2⧈	2▫	5◘	10■	2▫	2⧈	1▫	2⧈	3▫	1					
31	1	3▫	1⧈	1▫	4◘	10■	2⧈	3▫	2⧈	3▫	1					
32	①	4▫	2⧈	3◘	10■	2⧈	2▫	2⧈	4▫	①						
33		②	3▫	5◘	10■	9▫	②									
34			③	3▫	4◘	10■	8▫	③								
35				④	3▫	3◘	10■	7▫	④							
36					⑤	2▫	3◘	9■	7▫	⑤						

FRINGE

Row			
1	20▫	5○	
2	19▫	5○	
3	18▫	5○	
4	17▫	5○	
5	3▫	13◘	5○
6	15◘	5○	
7	11◘	4■	5○
8	10◘	5■	5○
9	8◘	7■	5○
10	6◘	9■	5○
11	15■	5○	
12	15■	5○	
13	15■	5○	
14	15■	5○	
15	15■	5○	
16	15■	5○	
17	15■	5○	
18	15■	5○	
19	9▫	6■	5○
20	11▫	4■	5○
21	14▫	1■	5○
22	15▫	5○	
23	15▫	5○	
24	15▫	5○	
25	15▫	5○	
26	16▫	5○	
27	17▫	5○	
28	18▫	5○	
29	19▫	5○	
30	20▫	5○	

● TECHNIQUE

1. Warp 32 threads.
2. Weave, pulling weft so panel is 4.5cm wide.
3. Fit to bar clip with 2 rows.
4. Weave the dress pattern on fringe.
5. Attach 30 strands of fringe.

卌 = Silver (TB558) 3g
○ = Gold (TB22) 2g
▲ = Dark Gold (TB221) 2g
× = Green (TB84) 2g
♯ = Yellow Green (TB775) 2g
◐ = Pink (TB54) 2g
⊙ = Gray (TB786) 2g
△ = Ivory (TB122) 2g
◎ = Orange (TB779) 2g
◘ = Light Purple (TB-425,783) 2g each
⧈ = Bluish Purple (TB788) 2g
▫ = Light Blue (TB328) 5g
■ = Black (TB49) 3g
● = Lavender (TB790) 2g

Flower Pendant

Pictured on page 8

● MATERIALS

Beads . . . . .Listed Below
Thread . . . . .Gray
Supplies . . . . .Gold Chain Set
Horizontal & Vertical Rows . . . . . .21 x 21
Warp Threads 22
Fringe . . . . .24 bds x 22

● TECHNIQUE

1. Warp 22 threads.
2. Put beads at the center of warp of 1st row, weave according to Stitch Number Sheet, and attach fringe.
3. Fringe: 8 Silver, 2 Gold (TB712), 1 Silver, 1 Gold, 1 Silver, 3 Gold, 3 Silver, 5 Gold (Picot)
4. Attach metal chain set with double thread.

= Silver (TB558) 4g
○ = Red (TB241) 20 bds
× = Light Pink (TB290) 20 bds
△ = Orange (TB791) 20 bds
◎ = Green (TB507) 20 bds
● = Light Blue (TB793) 20 bds

1	1									
2	3									
3	1	2◎	2							
4	4	1◎	2							
5	5	1◎	3							
6	5	4○	2							
7	5	2○	4△	2						
8	2	1●	1◎	2	1○	2△	2○	1△	3	
9	4	1●	1◎	1	1○	2△	1○	2×	1◎	3
10	5	1●	1◎	2	2△	1	1×	2●	1◎	3
11	7	5○	2	1◎	2●	4				
12	6	5×	2△	3	1●	2				
13	4	1△	1×	3△	2×	1△	5			
14	3	2△	2○	1△	2×	1△	4			
15	4	1○	2△	1×	2△	3				
16	3	1×	1◎	2×	4					
17	3	1◎	1●	4						
18	2	1●	4							
19	5									
20	3									
21	1									

Madam Fumi Pendant

Pictured on page 8

● MATERIALS

Beads . . . . .Listed Below
Thread . . . . .Gray
Horizontal & Vertical Rows . . . .29 x 33
Warp Threads 30
Fringe . . . . .29bds x 28

● TECHNIQUE

1. Warp 30 threads.
2. Reduce 6 beads from 1st row and 3 beads from 2nd row to shape the panel. In reverse manner reduce beads from row 30 to 33.
3. After reducing beads, to change the shape, attach 3 strands with 40 beads from the location of the change.

= Violet (TB771) 5g
□ = Gold (TB22) 2g
● = Light Blue (TB328) 1g
△ = Black (TB49) 20bds
○ = Yellow Grn (TB775) 1g
▲ = Orange (TB779) 20bds
▣ = Pink (TB780) 20bds
◎ = Ivory (TB123) 1g
◘ = Dark Gold (TB221) 1g
▽ = Purple (TB85) 4g
× = Green (TB507) 20bds
■ = Lavender (TB790) 20bds

1	⑥	17□	⑥										
2	③	3□	17	3□	③								
3	3□	23	3□										
4	1□	27	1□										
5	1□	6	4●	1▲	2○	4△	2○	8	1□				
6	1□	6	3●	1▲	3×	2△	2○	10	1□				
7	1□	5	3●	1▲	2△	2○	3▣	1×	3■	2×	5	1□	
8	1□	4	3●	1▲	3△	2○	3▣	2×	2■	2○	5	1□	
9	1□	3	4●	2▲	2△	3▲	2▣	1○	2▲	1■	2○	5	1□
10	1□	5	2●	2◘	3▲	3■	3▲	4△	5	1□			
11	1□	2	4●	5◘	4▲	2	2▲	4△	4	1□			
12	1□	1	5●	7◘	3▲	3	1▲	3△	4	1□			
13	1□	3	4●	8◘	2▲	2	3▲	5	1□				
14	1□	4	3●	7◘	3◎	4▲	6	1□					
15	1□	3	3●	7◘	3◎	2●	2◎	7	1□				
16	1□	1	4●	8◘	1□	6◎	7	1□					
17	1□	3	2●	6◘	2◎	1□	7◎	6	1□				
18	1□	3	3●	4◘	12◎	5	1□						
19	1□	6	4●	9◎	8	1□							
20	1□	6	3●	9◎	9	1□							
21	1□	4	3●	1▽	10◎	9	1□						
22	1□	3	4●	2▽	6◎	6●	6	1□					
23	1□	2	4●	4▽	1□	4◎	3●	9	1□				
24	1□	1	3●	6▽	1◎	1□	2◎	1□	1▽	3●	8	1□	
25	1□	1	2●	8▽	1◎	2□	2◎	2●	1▽	8	1□		
26	1□	2●	9▽	5◎	2▽	9	1□						
27	1□	1●	11▽	5◎	2▽	8	1□						
28	1□	1●	12▽	4◎	3▽	7	1□						
29	1□	20▽	7	1□									
30	①	1□	20▽	5	1□	①							
31	②	1□	19▽	4	1□	②							
32	③	1□	19▽	3	1□	③							
33	④	21□	④										

Butterfly Choker

Pictured on page 10

● MATERIALS

Beads . . . . .Black 20g, Gold 1g, Dark Gold 1g
Thread . . . . .Black
Supplies . . . . .Gold Necklace Finding
Horizontal & Vertical Rows . . . . .19 x 21
Warp Threads 20

● TECHNIQUE

1. Weave pattern of butterfly in 19 stitches x 21 rows.
2. Cross warps on right and left sides in panel.
3. Put warps through the required number of beads.
4. Attach findings as illustrated.

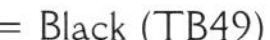

= Black (TB49)
▲ = Gold (TB712)
● = Dark Gold (TB221)

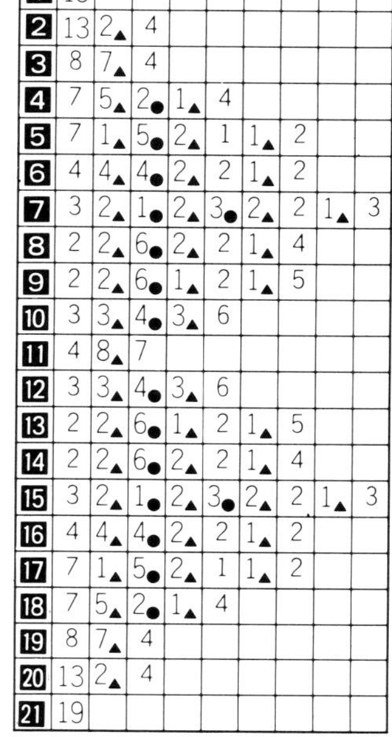

1	19								
2	13	2▲	4						
3	8	7▲	4						
4	7	5▲	2●	1▲	4				
5	7	1▲	5●	2▲	1	1▲	2		
6	4	4▲	4●	2▲	2	1▲	2		
7	3	2▲	1●	2▲	3●	2▲	2	1▲	3
8	2	2▲	6●	2▲	2	1▲	4		
9	2	2▲	6●	1▲	2	1▲	5		
10	3	3▲	4●	3▲	6				
11	4	8▲	7						
12	3	3▲	4●	3▲	6				
13	2	2▲	6●	1▲	2	1▲	5		
14	2	2▲	6●	2▲	2	1▲	4		
15	3	2▲	1●	2▲	3●	2▲	2	1▲	3
16	4	4▲	4●	2▲	2	1▲	2		
17	7	1▲	5●	2▲	1	1▲	2		
18	7	5▲	2●	1▲	4				
19	8	7▲	4						
20	13	2▲	4						
21	19								

Rose Choker

Pictured on page 10

Rose is designed in 21 stitches x 21 rows. The weaving method is the same as the butterfly. The design at choker section can be changed as desired.

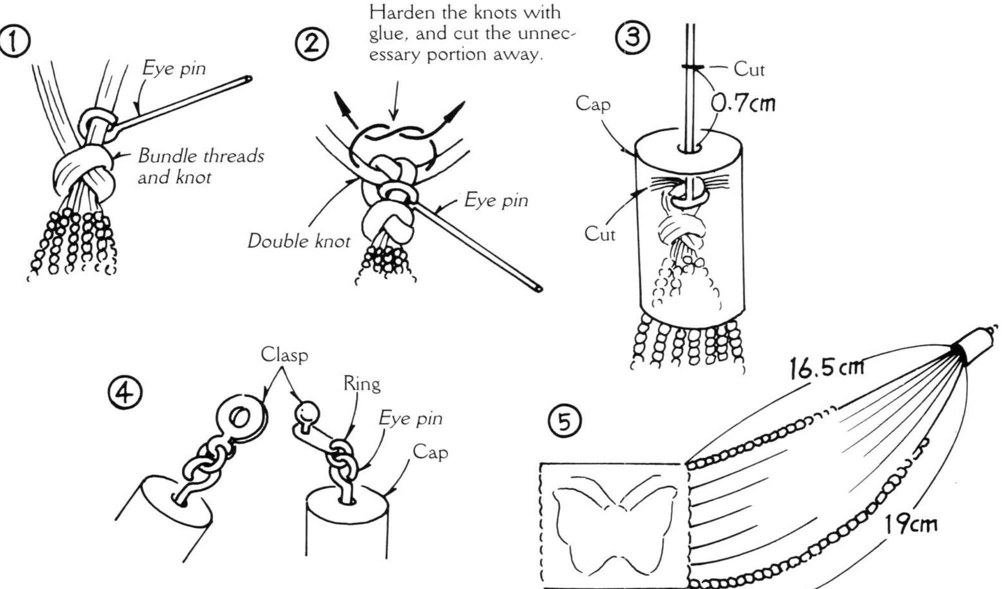

Paisley Brooch

Pictured on page 7

● MATERIALS

Beads . . .Frosted Blue(FB) 16g, Dark Gold(DG) 8g, Gold(G) 7g
Thread . . . . .Gray
Supplies . . . . . . .Felt or Leather, Safety Pin, 6cm Metal Finding
Horizontal & Vertical Rows . . . . .41 x 67
Warp Threads 42
Fringe . . . . .45bds x 42
10 DG, 2 FB, 4 G, 2 FB, 2 G, 2 DG, 8 FB, 10 G, 5 G (Picot)

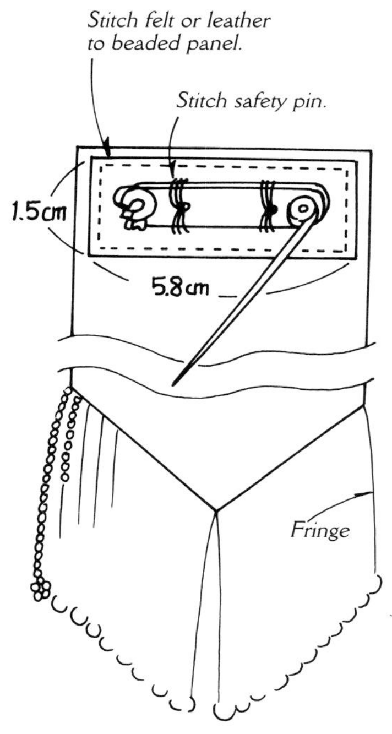

Row																							
1	18	1●	7	1●	14																		
2	17	1●	1	2●	3	4●	3	6●	4														
3	10	1●	5	1●	4	1●	1	1●	3	2●	2	6●	4										
4	9	2●	5	1●	1	1×	2	8●	1×	3	4●	4											
5	8	4●	3	1●	1	1×	1	2×	1	1●	5	2●	4	4●	3								
6	8	4●	1	1●	1	1×	1	1×	3	1●	5	4●	4	2●	4								
7	7	2●	3	1●	1	1●	2	1×	4	1●	2	1×	1	6●	8								
8	7	1●	2	1×	2	2●	1	5●	1	1●	2	2●	5	4●	5								
9	6	1●	1	1×	4	2●	1×	1	1●	3	4●	9	4●	3									
10	5	1●	7	1×	3	1●	4	2●	1	1●	15												
11	4	2●	1	1×	4	1●	4	1●	3	2●	2	1×	15										
12	4	1●	5	9●	1	1●	3	2●	4	7●	4												
13	4	1●	1	1×	2	1●	2	1●	4	4●	2	1●	1	1●	1	3●	6	1●	4				
14	4	1●	3	1●	3	1●	4	2●	2	2●	2	3●	3	2×	2	1●	5						
15	4	1●	1	1×	1	1●	3	1●	2	3●	2	3●	2	2●	3	2×	2	2●	5				
16	4	1●	2	1●	5	1●	1	2●	2	2●	2	1●	3	3×	3	2●	6						
17	2●	2	2●	1	9●	2	2●	2	2×	1	3×	3	3●	7									
18	2●	3	3●	6	1●	2	1●	3	5×	3	3●	9											
19	1●	1	2●	1	2●	3	4●	2	1●	3	5×	6	2●	8									
20	1●	3	3●	3	1●	1	2●	1	1●	3	8×	5	3●	1	2●	3							
21	1●	1	1×	2	1●	3	5●	1	1●	2	7×	5	3●	3	3●	2							
22	1●	4	1●	4	4●	1	1●	3	4×	4	3●	4	3●	4									
23	1●	1	1×	2	1●	3	2●	1	2●	1	2●	8	2●	4	4●	6							
24	1●	4	1●	1	2●	2	1×	1	2●	1	9●	4	3●	1	1●	1	1●	5					
25	1●	1	1×	2	1●	1	1●	5	2●	11	6●	1	1●	3	2●	2							
26	1●	2	1×	1	14●	3	6●	1	1×	2	1●	4	2●	2									
27	1	1●	3	1●	5	1●	1	2×	1	7●	1×	1	1×	1	2●	1×	2	1●	3	2●	3		
28	2	4●	4	2●	1	2×	1	1●	2	1×	2	1●	2	1×	1	1●	1	2●	1	1●	2	2●	4
29	4	4●	2	1●	3	3●	2	1×	1	1●	1	1●	3	1●	3	4●	6						
30	5	3●	2	1●	1	3●	1	1●	3	2●	2	4●	3	1●	3	1×	1	1×	3				
31	4	10●	3	1●	2	1●	5	1●	1	2●	1×	6	1×	3									
32	3	2●	2	1×	2	2●	6	2●	4	4●	2	1×	5	1×	4								
33	3	1●	2	3×	3	12●	3	1●	1×	3	1×	1	1×	3	2●	1							
34	4●	2	2×	4	2●	1	1×	7	1×	3	1●	1	2●	4	3●	3							

= Frosted Blue (TB705)
● = Dark Gold (TB221)
× = Gold (TB712)

Family Crest Mini Pouch

Pictured on page 13

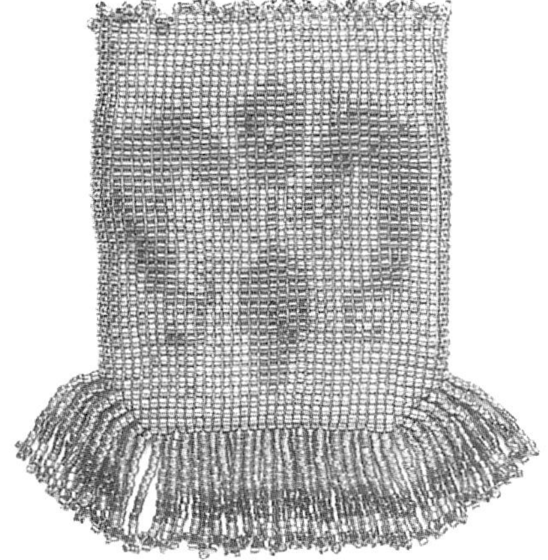

● MATERIALS

Beads . . . . .Nickel(N) 20g, Wine(W) 4g, Charcoal(C) 1g
Thread . . . . .Gray
Supplies . . . . .Small hook,
Lining: Wine Satin 20cm x 10cm
Horizontal & Vertical Rows . . . . .39 x 41
Warp Threads . . . . .60cm x 40
Fringe . . . . .17bds x 52
8N, 1 W, 3 C, 2N, 3 W (Picot)

= Nickel (TB711)
○ = Wine Red (TB332)
× = Charcoal Gray (TB90)

1	39														
2	39														
3	39														
4	39														
5	39														
6	39														
7	19	1○	19												
8	18	3○	18												
9	17	5○	17												
10	8	3○	5	3○	1×	3○	5	3○	8						
11	6	6○	4	3○	1×	3○	4	6○	6						
12	4	9○	3	3○	1×	3○	3	9○	4						
13	3	11○	2	3○	1×	3○	2	11○	3						
14	3	12○	1	3○	1×	3○	1	12○	3						
15	3	12○	2	2○	1×	2○	2	12○	3						
16	3	7○	1	4○	2	5○	2	4○	1	7○	3				
17	3	6○	3	3○	3	3○	3	3○	3	6○	3				
18	3	6○	5	2○	7	2○	5	6○	3						
19	3	5○	7	1○	3	1×	3	1○	7	5○	3				
20	4	4○	5	1○	1	1○	3	1×	3	1○	1	1○	5	4○	4
21	4	4○	6	1○	4	1×	4	1○	6	4○	4				
22	4	4○	23	4○	4										
23	5	3○	11	1○	11	3○	5								
24	5	4○	9	3○	9	4○	5								
25	5	4○	8	2○	1×	2○	8	4○	5						
26	6	3○	7	3○	1×	3○	7	3○	6						
27	6	4○	6	3○	1×	3○	6	4○	6						
28	8	4○	4	3○	1×	3○	4	4○	8						
29	10	2○	4	3○	1×	3○	4	2○	10						
30	11	1○	4	3○	1×	3○	4	1○	11						
31	8	1○	2	1○	4	3○	1×	3○	4	1○	2	1○	8		
32	8	4○	5	2○	1×	2○	5	4○	8						
33	17	2○	1×	2○	17										
34	18	1○	1×	1○	18										
35	18	3○	18												
36	①	17	3○	17	①										
37	②	17	1○	17	②										
38	③	33	③												
39	④	31	④												
40	⑤	29	⑤												
41	⑥	27	⑥												

35	3	1●	1	1×	5	3●	2	1×	7	1×	2	1●	4	4●	5	
36	1●	2	1●	3	5●	2	1●	3	1×	6	1×	2	1●	12		
37	9●	5	2●	3	1×	1	1×	1	1×	5	1●	11				
38	1●	6	1●	8	2●	10	4●	9								
39	1●	5	3●	8	11●	13										
40	1●	2	1●	2	2●	7	7●	8	3●	8						
41	1	3●	2	2●	4	3●	2	1×	1	2●	1	2●	4	5●	8	
42	5●	1	2●	4	1●	3	1×	1	1●	2	2●	4	1●	13		
43	1●	3	1●	1	2●	2	2●	3	1×	1	1●	3	2●	6	1●	11
44	5	2●	2	2●	4	1×	1	1●	2	1●	3	2●	4	4●	7	
45	8	2●	5	1×	2●	2	1●	3	2●	8	3●	4				
46	8	1●	4	1●	1	1×	1	1●	3	1●	2	1●	1	8●	7	
47	8	1●	3	2●	1	1×	1	1●	3	3●	4	3●	10			
48	①	6	2●	3	2●	1	1×	1	1●	22	①					
49	②	5	1●	3	1●	1	1●	1	1×	1	1●	21	②			
50	③	4	1●	3	1●	1	1●	1	1×	1	2●	19	③			
51	④	3	1●	2	1●	2	1●	1	1×	2	2●	17	④			
52	⑤	2	1●	2	1●	2	1●	1	1×	3	2●	15	⑤			
53	⑥	1	2●	1	1●	2	1●	1	2×	4	2●	12	⑥			
54	⑦	1	1●	1	1●	2	1●	2	2×	4	7●	5	⑦			
55	⑧	1●	1	1●	3	2●	1	3×	13	⑧						
56	⑨	1	1●	4	2●	2	7×	6	⑨							
57	⑩	6	4●	11	⑩											
58	⑪	8	6●	5	⑪											
59	⑫	17	⑫													
60	⑬	15	⑬													
61	⑭	13	⑭													
62	⑮	11	⑮													
63	⑯	9	⑯													
64	⑰	7	⑰													
65	⑱	5	⑱													
66	⑲	3	⑲													
67	⑳	1	⑳													

Parasol Brooch

Pictured on page 11

● MATERIALS

Beads .... Listed Below
Thread .... Gray
Supplies .... Corsage Pin
Horizontal & Vertical Rows, Parasol .... 52 x 39
Horizontal & Vertical Rows, Handle .... 7 x 74
Warp Threads 53
Fringe .... 10bds x 52
8 Purple, 2 Gold

PARASOL

● TECHNIQUE

1. Complete panel and then stitch the sides to make it in the form of umbrella and attach 52 fringes.
2. Stitch the side of handle panel.
3. Insert handle into the umbrella panel, secure it, and attach brooch pin.

1	⑩	32○		⑩																						
2	⑨	34○		⑨																						
3	⑧	2○	16	3△	6	2×	5	2○		⑧																
4	⑦	2○	5	2△	3	2△	2	3×	6	5△	1×	5	2○		⑦											
5	⑤	2○	2	1×	3	2×	5▲	2△	1	2×	3□	3	2□	3△	9	2○		⑤								
6	④	2○	2	3×	1	2×	3▲	2○	2▲	1△	2	1△	4□	2◎	1	1□	1×	6	2▲	4	2○		④			
7	②	2○	2	1×	3△	1×	1	2×	1△	4▲	6	1△	3□	1◎	2	1□	2×	4	4▲	1	2×	2	2○		②	
8	①	2○	3	1×	3△	1×	3	1×	4▲	1×	4	3△	3□	1	1□	3△	1×	2	3▲	1○	2▲	2×	3	2○		①
9		2○	2	3◎	4△	1×	1	2×	3△	2×	4	1×	3△	4□	3△	1×	2	2▲	2○	2▲	3×	3	2○			
10		3	2◎	2	2◎	3△	1	4×	1	1×	5	1×	3△	1	4△	2×	4	4▲	2×	1	2×	4				
11	①	1	1×	4◎	1	2◎	1	1×	1	2△	10	3△	2	3△	8	3×	2	2×	3		①					
12	②	1×	2◎	1○	4◎	1×	10	3●	2	1×	1	3△	10	2×	3	2×	2		②							
13	③	1◎	4	1◎	3△	2	3▲	4	3●	4	3▲	4	3●	3	1×	5	1×	1		③						
14	④	4◎	4△	2	3▲	4	3●	4	3▲	4	3●	10		④												
15	⑤	2	3●	4	3▲	18	3●	4	3▲	2		⑤														
16	⑥	1	3●	8	16○	8	3▲	1		⑥																
17	⑥	1	3●	7	18○	7	3▲	1		⑥																
18	⑦	9	2○	6⧖	2×	8⧖	2○	9		⑦																
19	⑧	7	2○	4⧖	1×	2⧖	2×	4⧖	1▲	4⧖	2○	7		⑧												
20	⑧	6	2○	4⧖	2×	1⧖	3△	2⧖	2●	2△	1⧖	2□	1⧖	2○	6		⑧									
21	⑨	4	2○	2⧖	2△	3×	1⧖	3△	1×	2●	3△	4□	1⧖	2○	4		⑨									
22	⑩	2	2○	4⧖	3△	4□	1△	1×	1⧖	1△	2▲	1△	4□	1⧖	1×	2○	2		⑩							
23	⑪	2○	2⧖	1×	2⧖	3△	4□	1△	1×	1⧖	1▲	1○	1□	1⧖	3□	3△	1	2○		⑪						
24	⑫	3⧖	2×	1⧖	2□	1⧖	4●	1×	2⧖	1▲	1○	1⧖	1▲	3●	3△	2⧖		⑫								
25	⑬	2⧖	3△	3□	4●	3□	1⧖	2▲	1⧖	3●	1⧖	1△	2⧖		⑬											
26	⑭	2⧖	2△	3□	2⧖	2●	4□	2×	2⧖	2△	3⧖		⑭													
27	⑭	1⧖	2△	1⧖	2△	1⧖	1×	2⧖	1△	1□	2○	1□	2×	1⧖	3△	3⧖		⑭								
28	⑮	2△	2⧖	1△	1○	1△	1⧖	2△	2□	3×	1⧖	3△	3×		⑮											
29	⑯	3⧖	3△	1⧖	3⧖	1□	4⧖	2△	3⧖		⑯															
30	⑰	3⧖	6△	2⧖	1○	2⧖	2△	2⧖		⑰																
31	⑱	8△	1⧖	1△	3	1△	2⧖		⑱																	
32	⑱	2△	2◎	4△	1⧖	2△	1⧖	2△	2⧖		⑱															
33	⑲	1⧖	2◎	10	1◎		⑲																			
34	⑳	2◎	6△	2◎	1△	1◎		⑳																		
35	㉑	2△	1◎	5△	2◎		㉑																			
36	㉑	2△	2◎	5△	1◎		㉑																			
37	㉒	2◎	6△		㉒																					
38	㉓	6△		㉓																						
39	㉔	4△		㉔																						

= Purple (TB461) 6g
○ = Gold (TB712) 2g
△ = Green (TB507) 2g
× = Yellow Green (TB775) 2g
□ = Purplish Red (TB785) 2g
▲ = Blue (TB781) 2g
● = Orange (TB-789) 2g
◎ = Dark Gold (TB221) 2g
⧖ = Light Brown (TB429) 2g

PARASOL HANDLE

1	7○
2	7
⌇	
6	7
7	7○
8	7
⌇	
12	7
13	7○
14	7
⌇	
18	7
19	7○
20	7
⌇	
24	7
25	7○
26	7
⌇	
80	7

Antique Pouch *Pictured on page 13*

● MATERIALS

Beads . . . . .Listed on chart, page 88
Thread . . . . .Gray
Supplies . . . . .Lining: 2 pieces, White Satin 30cm x 40cm
Horizontal & Vertical Rows: A . . . . .2 panels, 61 x140
Horizontal & Vertical Rows: B . . . . .2 panels, 61 x139
Warp Threads A-62; B-62
Straps . . . . .2 straps, 7 x 200

● TECHNIQUE

1. Weave 2 panels of A and B respectively, Sew the 4 panels together.
2. Attach fringe and then straps.
3. Stitch lining cloth.
4. Put elastic through to complete.

Wild Rose Pouch *Pictured on page 16*

● MATERIALS

Beads . . . . .Listed on chart, page 90
Thread . . . . .Gray
Supplies . . . . .Lining: Black Satin 30cm x 40cm
. . . . .Black fastener
Horizontal & Vertical Rows: Bag . . . . .126 x 88
Horizontal & Vertical Rows: Strap . . . . .7 x 105cm
Warp Threads 127

● TECHNIQUE

1. Warp 127 threads.
2. Weave panels according to chart.
3. Pull warps after weaving to finish. Fold the panels in two, and stitch the sides.
4. Close inner bag and attach fastener.
5. Weave strap about 105cm long in 7 stitches (1 Black, 2 Frosted Brown, 1 Black, 2 Frosted brown, 1 Black) and stitch on both sides.

= Mix (TB201 & TB712) 140g
× = Nickel (TB711) 10g
○ = Silver (TB21) 23g
△ = Green (TB507) 6g
● = Gold (TB712) 20g

1. WEAVE 2 PANELS OF PATTERNS A AND B RESPECTIVELY.

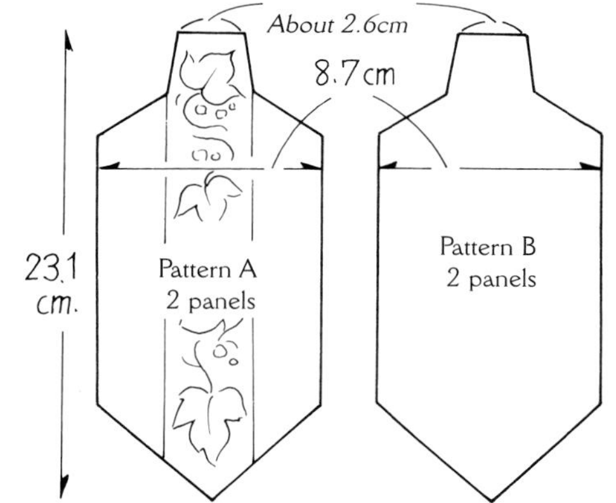

2. FRINGE POSITION

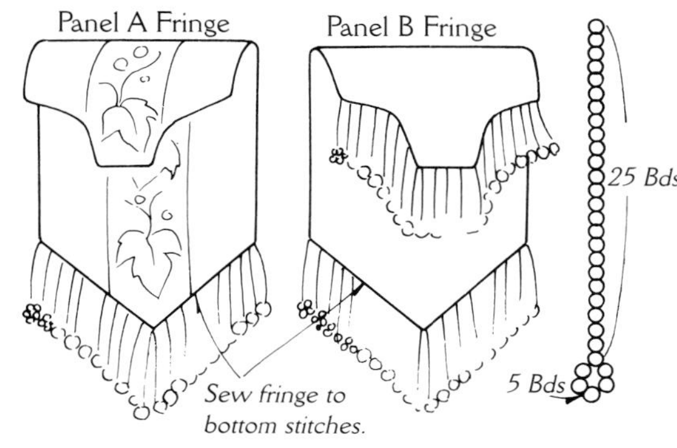

3. HOW TO MAKE INNER BAG

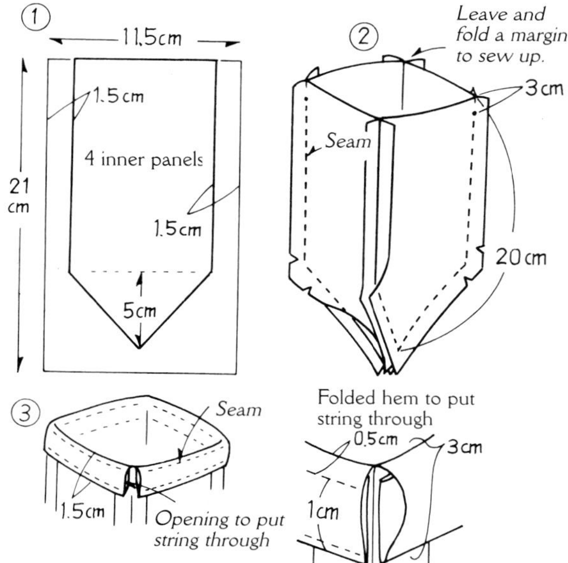

STITCH CHART FOR *ANTIQUE POUCH* PANEL A

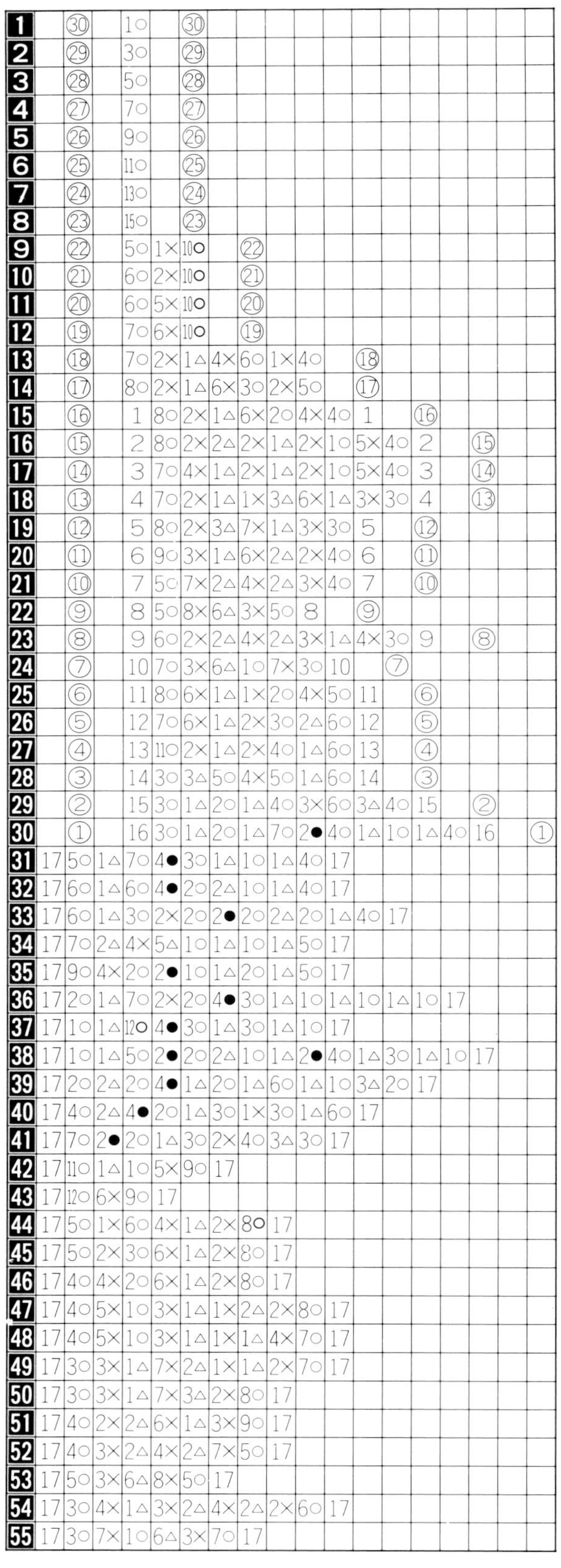

Row																		
1		㉚		1○		㉚												
2		㉙		3○		㉙												
3		㉘		5○		㉘												
4		㉗		7○		㉗												
5		㉖		9○		㉖												
6		㉕		11○		㉕												
7		㉔		13○		㉔												
8		㉓		15○		㉓												
9		㉒		5○	1×	10○		㉒										
10		㉑		6○	2×	10○		㉑										
11		⑳		6○	5×	10○		⑳										
12		⑲		7○	6×	10○		⑲										
13		⑱		7○	2×	1△	4×	6○	1×	4○		⑱						
14		⑰		8○	2×	1△	6×	3○	2×	5○		⑰						
15		⑯		1	8○	2×	1△	6×	2○	4×	4○	1		⑯				
16		⑮		2	8○	2×	2△	2×	1△	2×	1○	5×	4○	2		⑮		
17		⑭		3	7○	4×	1△	2×	1△	2×	1○	5×	4○	3		⑭		
18		⑬		4	7○	2×	1△	1×	3△	6×	1△	3×	3○	4		⑬		
19		⑫		5	8○	2×	3△	7×	1△	3×	3○	5		⑫				
20		⑪		6	9○	3×	1△	6×	2△	2×	4○	6		⑪				
21		⑩		7	5○	7×	2△	4×	2△	3×	4○	7		⑩				
22		⑨		8	5○	8×	6△	3×	5○	8		⑨						
23		⑧		9	6○	2×	2△	4×	2△	3×	1△	4×	3○	9		⑧		
24		⑦		10	7○	3×	6△	1○	7×	3○	10		⑦					
25		⑥		11	8○	6×	1△	1×	2○	4×	5○	11		⑥				
26		⑤		12	7○	6×	1△	2×	3○	2△	6○	12		⑤				
27		④		13	11○	2×	1△	2×	4○	1△	6○	13		④				
28		③		14	3○	3△	5○	4×	5○	1△	6○	14		③				
29		②		15	3○	1△	2○	1△	4○	3×	6○	3△	4○	15		②		
30		①		16	3○	1△	2○	1△	7○	2●	4○	1△	1○	1△	4○	16		①
31	17	5○	1△	7○	4●	3○	1△	1○	1△	4○	17							
32	17	6○	1△	6○	4●	2○	2△	1○	1△	4○	17							
33	17	6○	1△	3○	2×	2○	2●	2○	2△	2○	1△	4○	17					
34	17	7○	2△	4×	5△	1○	1△	1○	1△	5○	17							
35	17	9○	4×	2○	2●	1○	1△	2○	1△	5○	17							
36	17	2○	1△	7○	2×	2○	4●	3○	1△	1○	1△	1○	1△	1○	17			
37	17	1○	1△	12○	4●	3○	1△	3○	1△	1○	17							
38	17	1○	1△	5○	2●	2○	2△	1○	1△	2●	4○	1△	3○	1△	1○	17		
39	17	2○	2△	2○	4●	1△	2○	1△	6○	1△	1○	3△	2○	17				
40	17	4○	2△	4●	2○	1△	3○	1×	3○	1△	6○	17						
41	17	7○	2●	2○	1△	3○	2×	4○	3△	3○	17							
42	17	11○	1△	1○	5×	9○	17											
43	17	12○	6×	9○	17													
44	17	5○	1×	6○	4×	1△	2×	8○	17									
45	17	5○	2×	3○	6×	1△	2×	8○	17									
46	17	4○	4×	2○	6×	1△	2×	8○	17									
47	17	4○	5×	1○	3×	1△	1×	2△	2×	8○	17							
48	17	4○	5×	1○	3×	1△	1×	1△	4×	7○	17							
49	17	3○	3×	1△	7×	2△	1×	1△	2×	7○	17							
50	17	3○	3×	1△	7×	3△	2×	8○	17									
51	17	4○	2×	2△	6×	1△	3×	9○	17									
52	17	4○	3×	2△	4×	2△	7×	5○	17									
53	17	5○	3×	6△	8×	5○	17											
54	17	3○	4×	1△	3×	2△	4×	2△	2×	6○	17							
55	17	3○	7×	1○	6△	3×	7○	17										

56	17	5○	4×	2○	1×	1△	6×	8○	17							
57	17	6○	2△	3○	2×	1△	6×	7○	17							
58	17	6○	1△	4○	2×	1△	2×	11○	17							
59	17	6○	1△	5○	4×	5○	3△	3○	17							
60	17	4○	3△	6○	3×	4○	1△	2○	1△	3○	17					
61	17	4○	1△	1○	1△	4○	2●	7○	1△	2○	1△	3○	17			
62	17	4○	1△	1○	1△	3○	4●	7○	1△	5○	17					
63	17	4○	1△	1○	2△	2○	4●	6○	1△	6○	17					
64	17	4○	1△	2○	2△	2○	2●	2○	2×	3○	1△	6○	17			
65	17	5○	1△	1○	1△	1○	5△	4×	2△	7○	17					
66	17	5○	1△	2○	1△	1○	2●	2○	4×	9○	17					
67	17	1○	1△	1○	1△	1○	1△	3○	4●	2○	2×	7○	1△	2○	17	
68	17	1○	1△	3○	1△	3○	4●	12○	1△	1○	17					
69	17	1○	1△	3○	1△	4○	2●	1△	1○	2△	2○	2●	5○	1△	1○	17
70	17	2○	3△	1○	1△	6○	1△	2○	1△	4●	2○	2△	2○	17		
71	17	6○	1△	3○	1×	3○	1△	2○	4●	2△	4○	17				
72	17	3○	3△	4○	2×	3○	1△	2○	2●	7○	17					
73	17	9○	5×	1○	1△	11	17									
74	17	9○	6×	12	17											
75	17	8○	2×	1△	4×	6○	1×	5○	17							
76	17	8○	2×	1△	6×	3○	2×	5○	17							
77	17	8○	2×	1△	6×	2○	4×	4○	17							
78	17	8○	2×	2△	2×	1△	2×	1○	5×	4○	17					
79	17	7○	4×	1△	2×	1△	2×	1○	5×	4○	17					
80	17	7○	2×	1△	1×	3△	6×	1△	3×	3○	17					
81	17	8○	2×	3△	7×	1△	3×	3○	17							
82	17	9○	3×	1△	6×	2△	2×	4○	17							
83	17	5○	7×	2△	4×	2△	3×	4○	17							
84	17	5○	8×	6△	3×	5○	17				17					
85	17	6○	2×	2△	4×	2△	3×	1△	4×	3○	17					
86	17	7○	3×	6△	1○	7×	3○	17								
87	17	8○	6×	1△	1×	2○	4×	5○	17							
88	17	7○	6×	1△	2×	3○	2△	6○	17							
89	17	11	2×	1△	2×	4○	1△	6○	17							
90	17	3○	3△	5○	4×	5○	1△	6○	17							
91	17	3○	1△	2○	1△	4○	3×	6○	3△	4○	17					
92	17	3○	1△	2○	1△	7○	2●	4○	1△	1○	1△	4○	17			
93	17	5○	1△	7○	4●	3○	1△	1○	1△	4○	17					
94	17	6○	1△	6○	4●	2○	2△	1○	1△	4○	17					
95	17	6○	1△	3○	2●	2○	2●	2○	2△	2○	1△	4○	17			
96	17	7○	2△	4●	5△	1○	1△	1○	1△	5○	17					
97	17	9○	4●	2○	2●	1○	1△	2○	1△	5○	17					
98	17	2○	1△	7○	2●	2○	4●	3○	1△	1○	1△	1○	1△	1○	17	
99	17	1○	1△	12○	4●	3○	1△	3○	1△	1○	17					
100	17	1○	1△	5○	2×	2○	2△	1○	1△	2●	4○	1△	3○	1△	1○	17
101	17	2○	2△	2○	4×	1△	2○	1△	6○	1△	1○	3△	2○	17		
102	17	4○	2△	4×	2○	1△	7○	1△	6○	17						
103	17	7○	2×	2○	1△	9○	3△	3○	17							
104	17	11○	1△	15○	17											
105	17	27○	17													
106	17	27○	17													
107	17	11○	1△	15○	17											
108	17	7○	2×	2○	1△	9○	3△	3○	17							
109	17	4○	2△	4×	2○	1△	7○	1△	6○	17						
110	17	2○	2△	2○	4×	1△	2○	1△	6○	1△	1○	3△	2○	17		
111	17	1○	1△	5○	2×	2○	2△	1○	1△	2●	4○	1△	3○	1△	1○	17

112	17	1○	1△	12○	4●	3○	1△	3○	1△	1○	17					
113	17	2○	1△	7○	2●	2○	4●	3○	1△	1○	1△	1○	1△	1○	17	
114	17	9○	4●	2○	2●	1○	1△	2○	1△	5○	17					
115	17	7○	2△	4●	5△	1○	1△	1○	1△	5○	17					
116	17	6○	1△	3○	2●	2○	2●	2○	2△	2○	1△	4○	17			
117	17	6○	1△	6○	4●	2○	2△	1○	1△	4○	17					
118	17	5○	1△	7○	4●	3○	1△	1○	1△	4○	17					
119	17	3○	1△	2○	1△	7○	2●	4○	1△	1○	1△	4○	17			
120	17	3○	1△	2○	1△	4○	3×	6○	3△	4○	17					
121	17	3○	3△	5○	4×	5○	1△	6○	17							
122	17	11○	2×	1△	2×	4○	1△	6○	17							
123	17	7○	6×	1△	2×	3○	2△	6○	17							
124		②	15	8○	6×	1△	1×	2○	4×	5○	15		②			
125		④	13	7○	3×	6△	1○	7×	3○	13		④				
126		⑥	11	6○	2×	2△	4×	2△	3×	1△	4×	3○	11		⑥	
127		⑧	9	5○	8×	6△	3×	5○	9		⑧					
128		⑩	7	5○	7×	2△	4×	2△	3×	4○	7		⑩			
129		⑫	5	9○	3×	1△	6×	2△	2×	4○	5		⑫			
130		⑭	3	8○	2×	3△	7×	1△	3×	3○	3		⑭			
131		⑯	1	7○	2×	1△	1×	3△	6×	1△	3×	3○	1		⑯	
132		⑯	1	7○	4×	1△	2×	1△	2×	1○	5×	4○	1		⑯	
133		⑰	8○	2×	2△	2×	1△	2×	1○	5×	4○		⑰			
134		⑰	8○	2×	1△	6×	2○	4×	4○		⑰					
135		⑱	7○	2×	1△	6×	3○	2×	4○		⑱					
136		⑱	7○	2×	1△	4×	6○	1×	4○		⑱					
137		⑲	7○	6×	10○		⑲									
138		⑲	7○	5×	11○		⑲									
139		⑳	7○	2×	12○		⑳									
140		㉑	6○	1×	12○		㉑									

CHART FOR *ANTIQUE POUCH* PANEL B

1		㉚		1		㉚
2		㉙		3		㉙
3		㉘		5		㉘
4		㉗		7		㉗
5		㉖		9		㉖
6		㉕		11		㉕
7		㉔		13		㉔
8		㉓		15		㉓
9		㉒		17		㉒
10		㉑		19		㉑
11		⑳		21		⑳
12		⑲		23		⑲
13		⑱		25		⑱
14		⑰		27		⑰
15		⑯		29		⑯
16		⑮		31		⑮
17		⑭		33		⑭
18		⑬		35		⑬
19		⑫		37		⑫
20		⑪		39		⑪
21		⑩		41		⑩
22		⑨		43		⑨
23		⑧		45		⑧
24		⑦		47		⑦
25		⑥		49		⑥

26		⑤		51		⑤
27		④		53		④
28		③		55		③
29		②		57		②
30		①		59		①
31		61				
⟆						
122		61				
123		②		57		②
124		④		53		④
125		⑥		49		⑥
126		⑧		45		⑧
127		⑩		41		⑩
128		⑫		37		⑫
129		⑭		33		⑭
130		⑯		29		⑯
131		⑯		29		⑯
132		⑰		27		⑰
133		⑰		27		⑰
134		⑱		25		⑱
135		⑱		25		⑱
136		⑲		23		⑲
137		⑲		23		⑲
138		⑳		21		⑳
139		㉑		19		㉑

Chart for Wild Rose Pouch

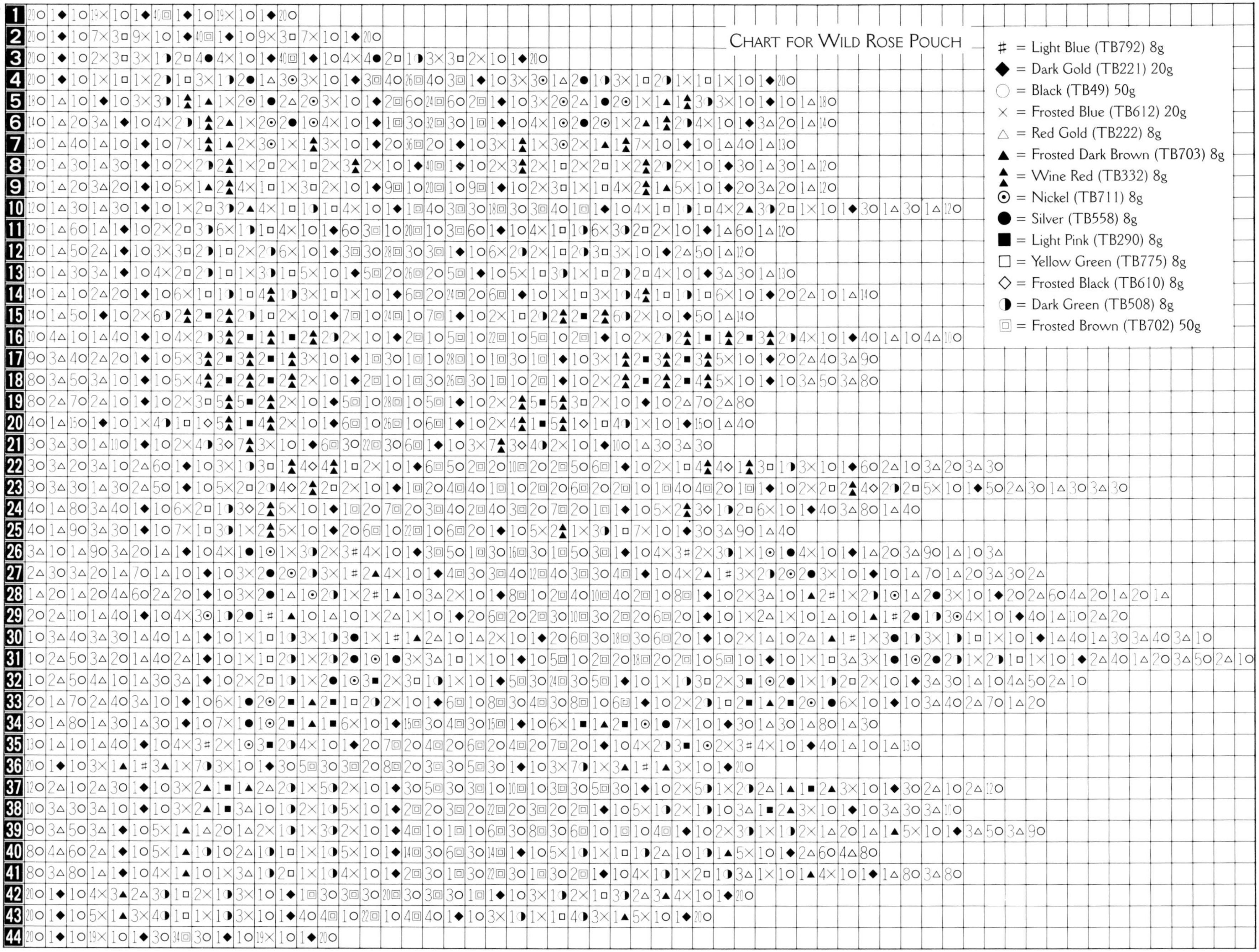

Symbol	Bead
#	= Light Blue (TB792) 8g
◆	= Dark Gold (TB221) 20g
○	= Black (TB49) 50g
×	= Frosted Blue (TB612) 20g
△	= Red Gold (TB222) 8g
▲	= Frosted Dark Brown (TB703) 8g
▲▲	= Wine Red (TB332) 8g
⊙	= Nickel (TB711) 8g
●	= Silver (TB558) 8g
■	= Light Pink (TB290) 8g
□	= Yellow Green (TB775) 8g
◇	= Frosted Black (TB610) 8g
◑	= Dark Green (TB508) 8g
⊡	= Frosted Brown (TB702) 50g

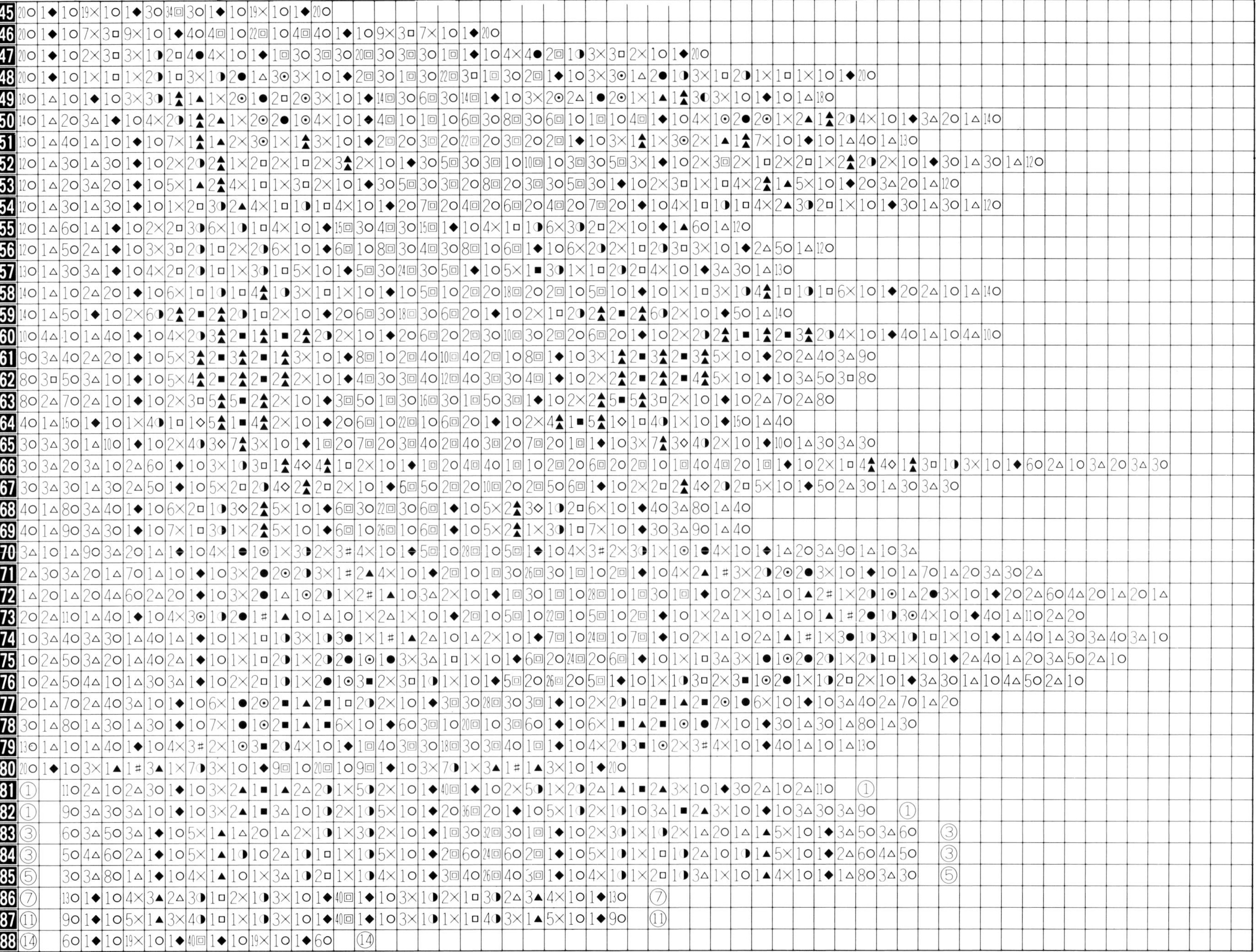

Initialed Pouch *Pictured on page 35*

Initials are made by mixing pure gold and black for high impact. A fringe is added for delight. By changing the base color stripes the pouch can be further personalized.
See pages 95-101 for Initial charts

Finished size: 14cm x 21cm

● MATERIALS

Beads . . . . .Nickel 100g, Gold 40g, Black 20g
Thread . . . . .Gray
Supplies . . . . .13cm closure
Lining:White satin, 20cm x 50 cm
Horizontal & Vertical Rows: Pouch . . . . .93 x 209
Horizontal & Vertical Rows: Strap . . . . .7 x 840 (120cm)
Fringe .28bds x 94 with 5 bead picot

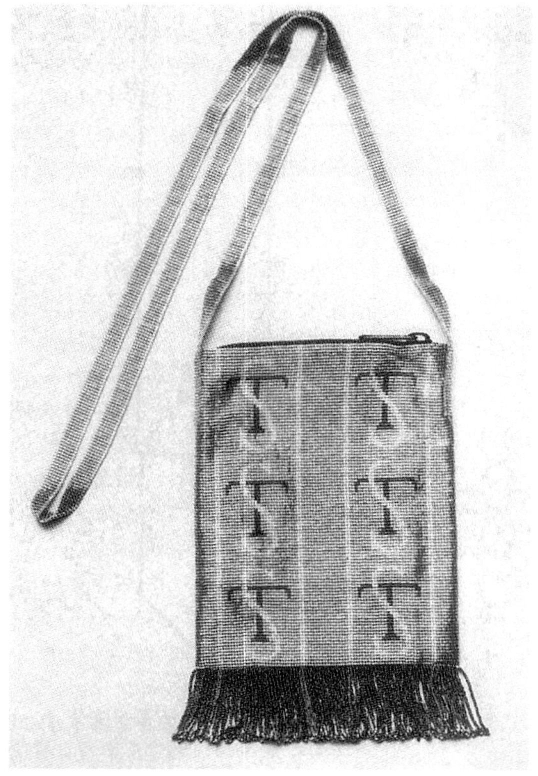

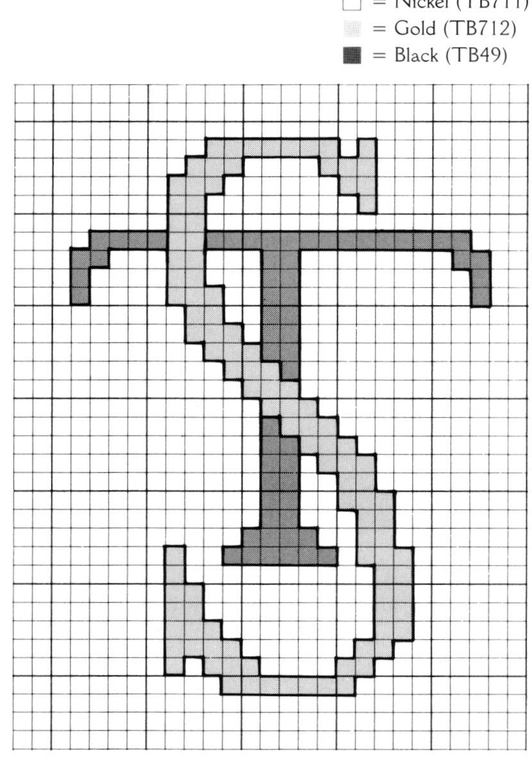

Spring Rhythm Choker

Pictured on page 19

Finished size: 2.7cm x 5cm

● MATERIALS

Beads . . . . Nickel 1g, Orange 3g
Thread . . . . Gray
Supplies . . . . Leather cord, Metal findings
Horizontal & Vertical Rows . . . . 13 x 12

STITCH CHART

Row					
1	13				
2	13				
3	13				
4	13				
5	13				
6	6	7●			
7	6	7●			
8	6	7●			
9	6	7●			
10	6	7●			
11	6	7●			
12	6	7●			

□ = Orange (TB779)
⊡ = Nickel (TB711)

How to read STITCH CHART
13 indicates 13 beads in orange
7● indicates 7 beads in nickel

FRINGE POSITION

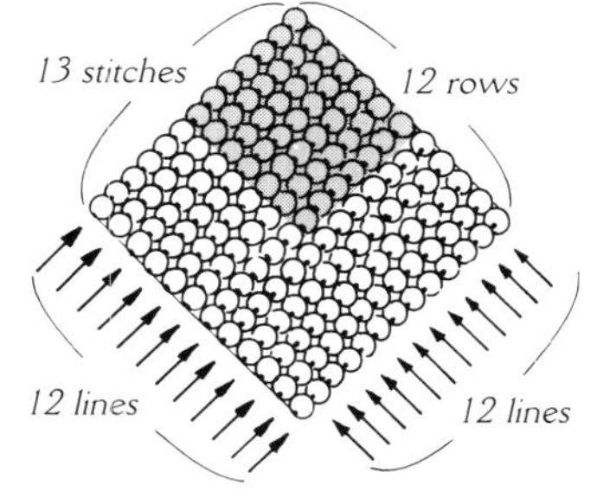

FRINGE BEADING

3 Bds Nickel
8 Bds Orange
2 Bds Nickel
2 Bds Orange
3 Bds Nickel

Emblem Initialed Brooch

Pictured on page 20

A decorative element on a jacket pocket, the emblem is arranged with a frosted black background, the "Y" in nickel and the "W" in brown. The metal fitting is of a pole type with traditional design.

Without fringes, the panel is finished by knotting the warp threads.

By attaching fringes a softer atmosphere is created.

The shooting star and crown are decorated with the appearance of stones around the panel.

Finished size: 4.5cm x 5cm

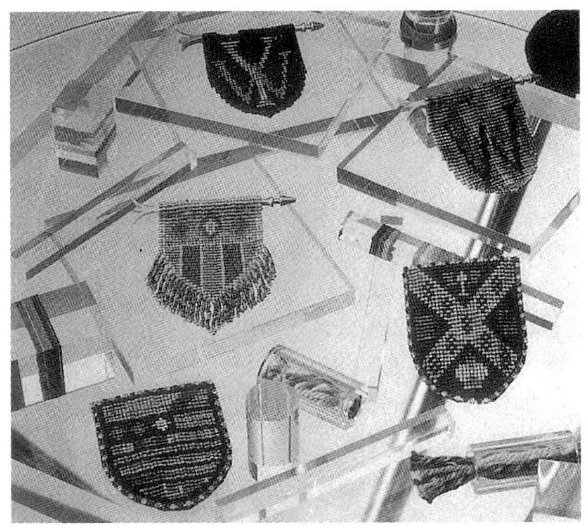

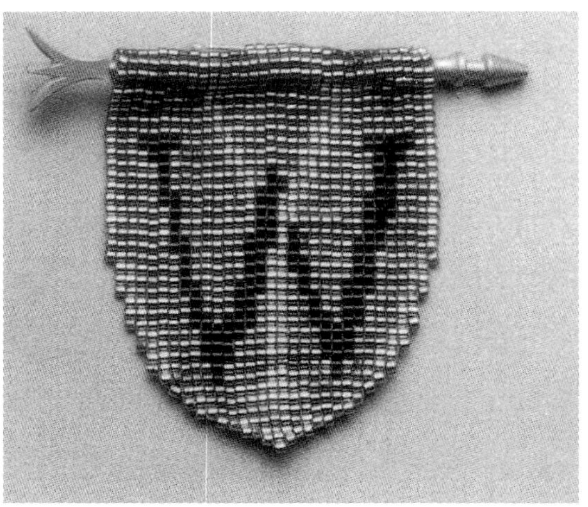

● MATERIALS

Beads . . . . . . .Nickel (TB711) 5g, Gold (TB712) 3g, Black (TB49) 2g
Thread . . . . .Black
Supplies . . . . .Arrow & Wing metal finding
Horizontal & Vertical Rows . . . . .31 x 38

This brooch has a nickel background color and letters in a combination of gold and black. The border is the same gold as the letter to create a simple elegant look.

Reduce the number of stitches in the weft to create a slight curve in the traditional emblem form.

Select appropriate initials and combine vertical and horizontal letters to form a monogram emblem.

● BASIC DESIGN

The initial letters can be drawn in various forms, but it is very important that the letters can be read clearly.

How to design

1. Take a copy of the two initials of family name and given name.
2. Overlap the two letters and decide the well-balanced position.
3. Decide color of the letters and draw an exact line between two letters.
4. Select background color to contrast the letter colors.
5. Draw a contour line for the emblem.

①

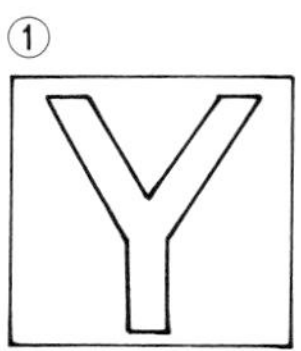

②

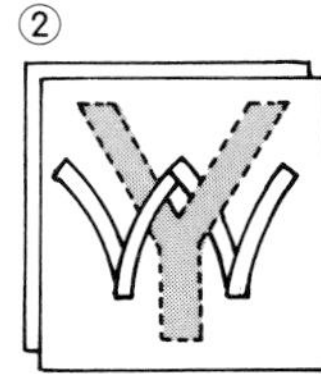

③

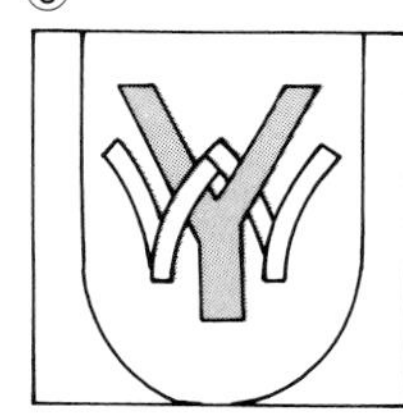

● TECHNIQUE

1. Arrange, making sure that the letters look beautiful and are balanced.

2. Even with the same design, the appearance will differ by using different color combinations, so make colors and lines clear.

3. It is interesting to explore letter combinations. Select 20 alphabetic letters and try 7 combinations as a reference.

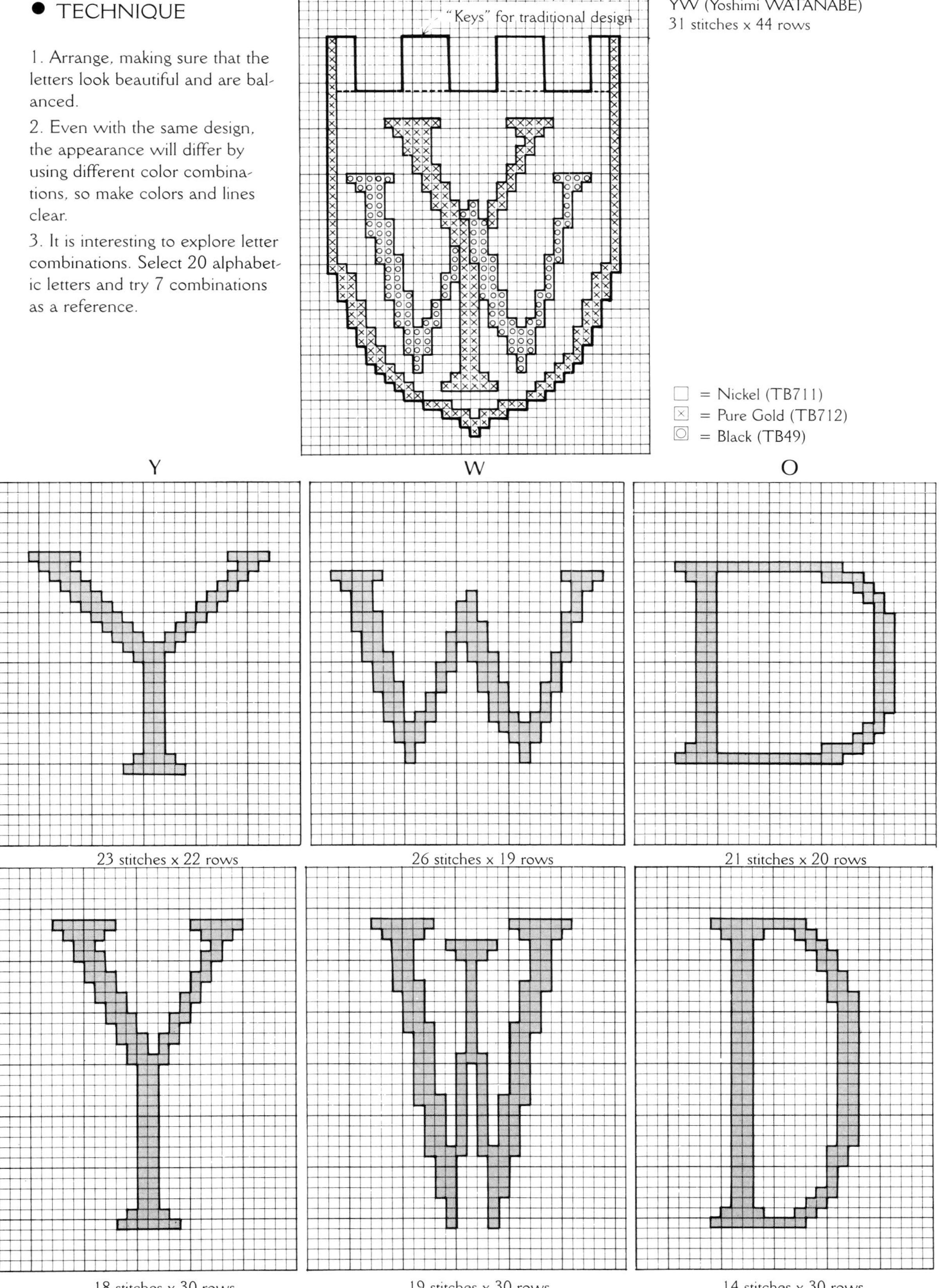

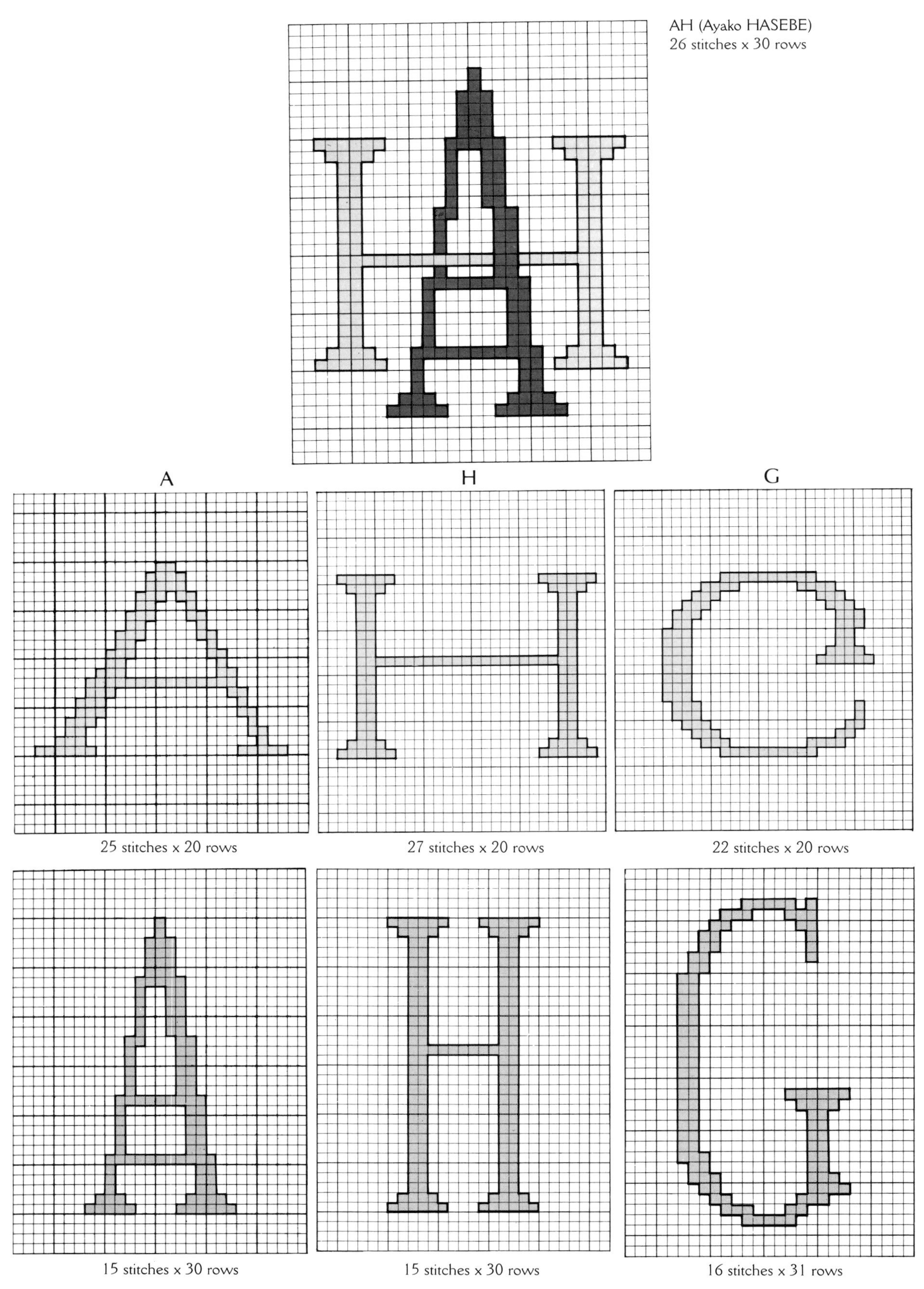

AH (Ayako HASEBE)
26 stitches x 30 rows

25 stitches x 20 rows

27 stitches x 20 rows

22 stitches x 20 rows

15 stitches x 30 rows

15 stitches x 30 rows

16 stitches x 31 rows

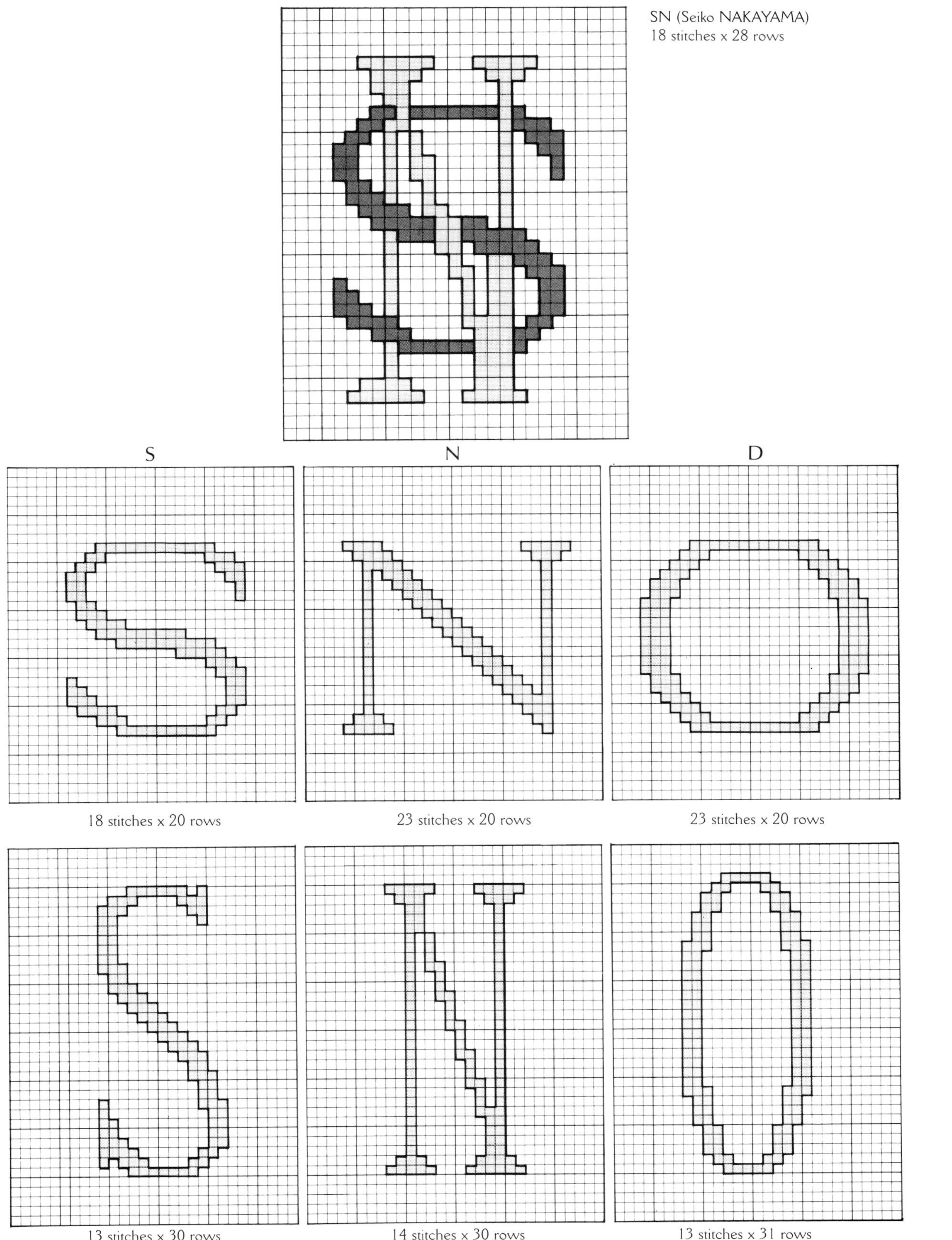
SN (Seiko NAKAYAMA)
18 stitches x 28 rows
S
N
D
18 stitches x 20 rows
23 stitches x 20 rows
23 stitches x 20 rows
13 stitches x 30 rows
14 stitches x 30 rows
13 stitches x 31 rows

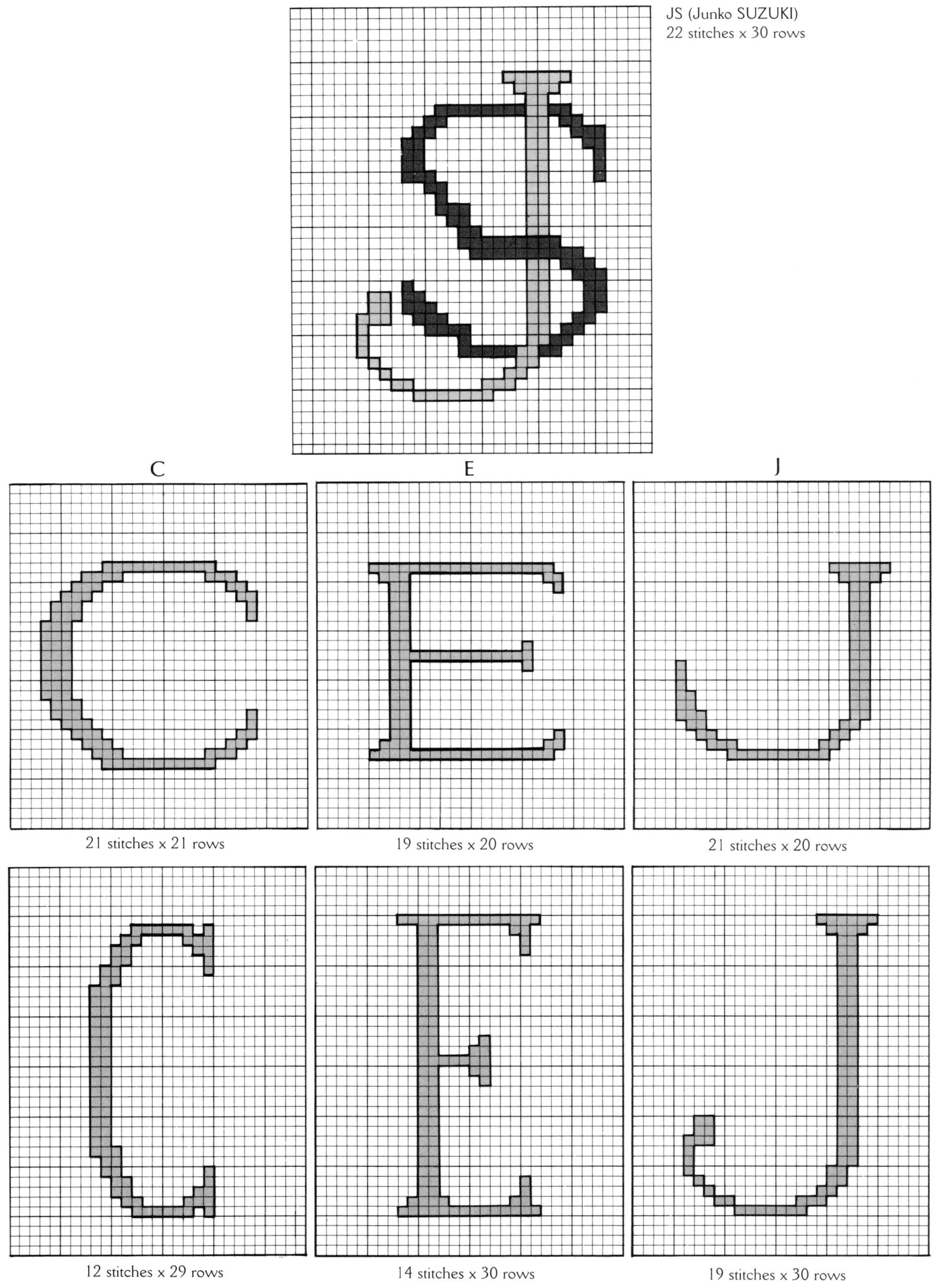
JS (Junko SUZUKI)
22 stitches x 30 rows
C
E
J
21 stitches x 21 rows
19 stitches x 20 rows
21 stitches x 20 rows
12 stitches x 29 rows
14 stitches x 30 rows
19 stitches x 30 rows

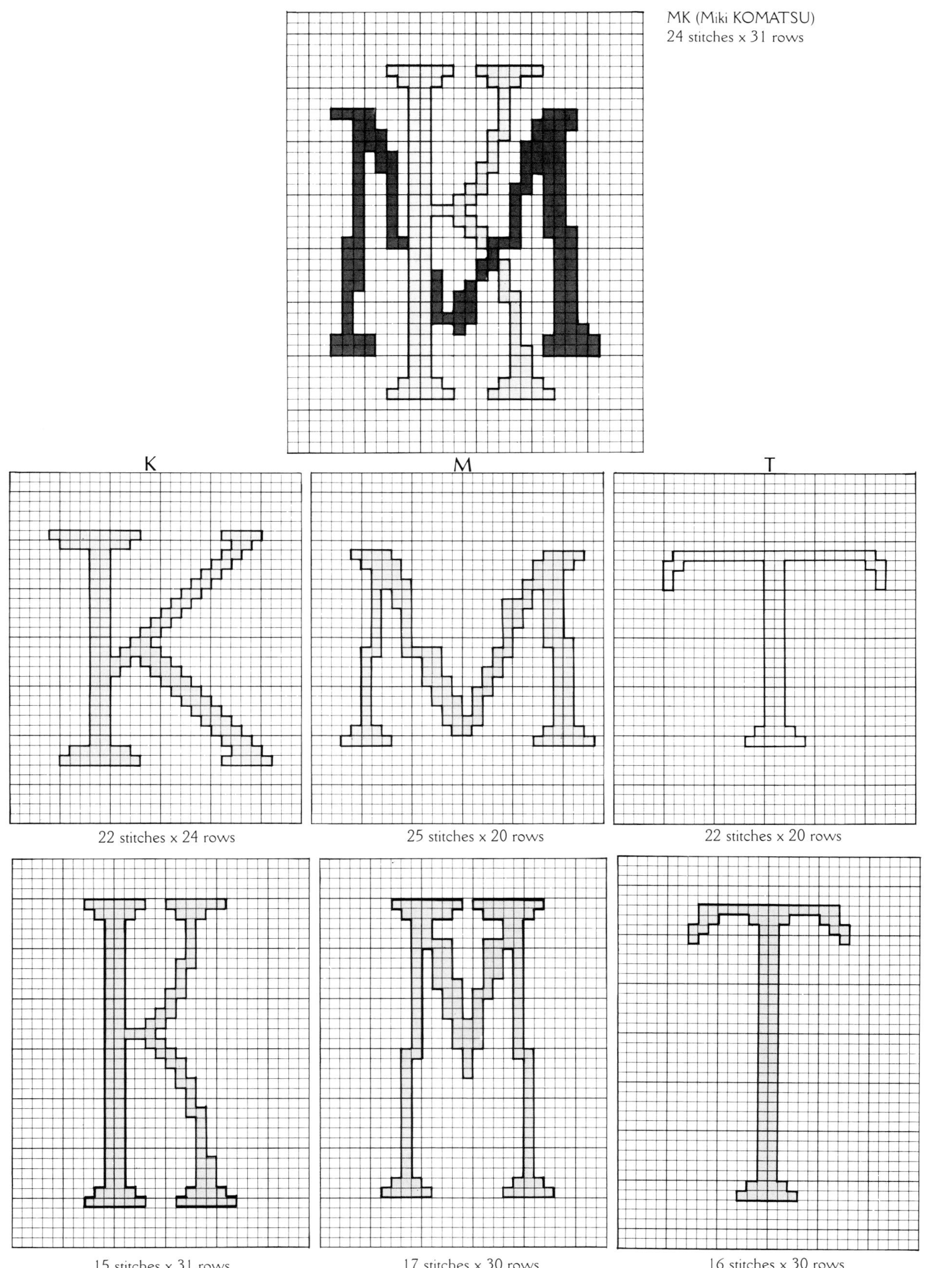

MK (Miki KOMATSU)
24 stitches x 31 rows
K
M
T
22 stitches x 24 rows
25 stitches x 20 rows
22 stitches x 20 rows
15 stitches x 31 rows
17 stitches x 30 rows
16 stitches x 30 rows

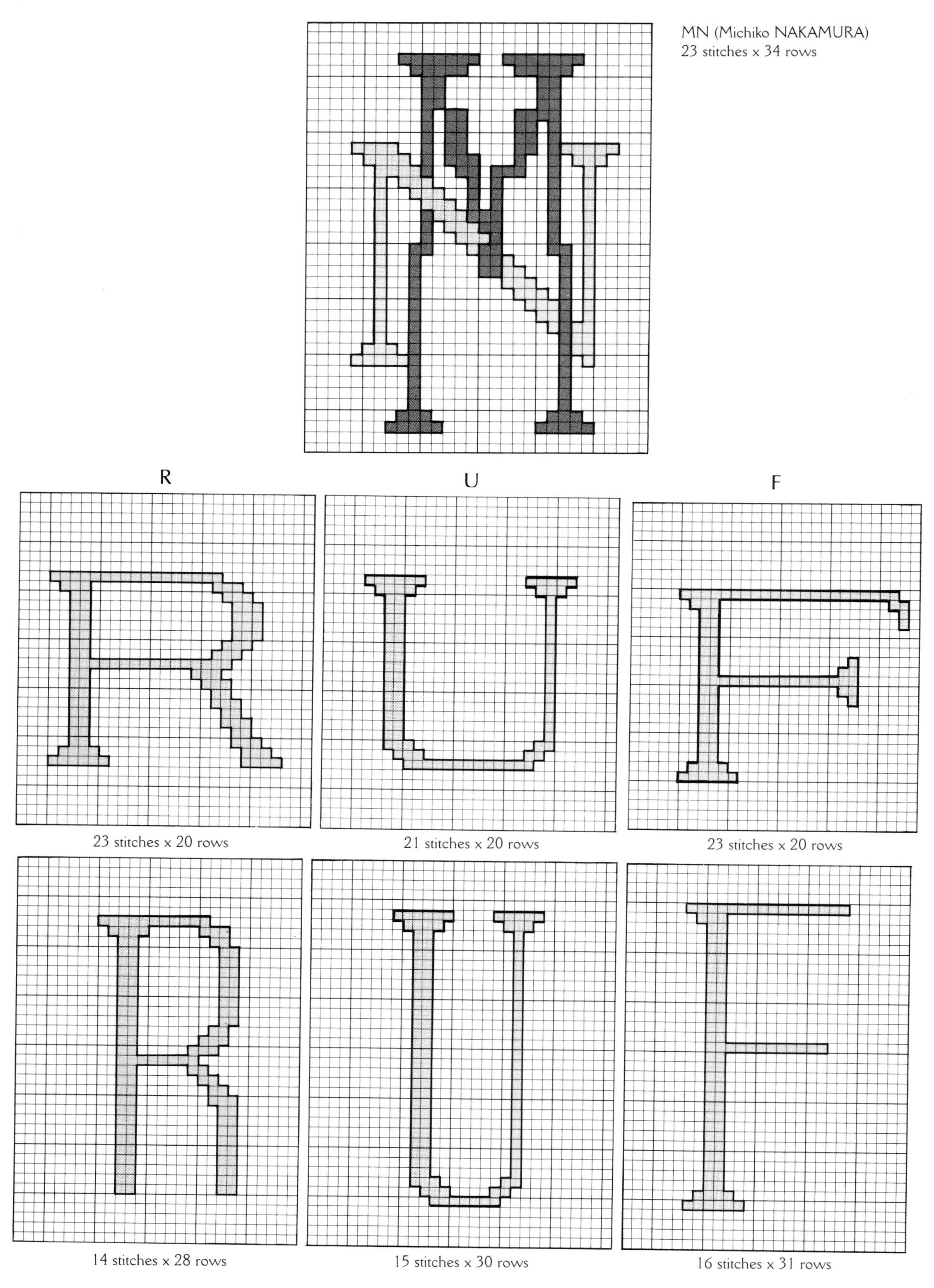

MN (Michiko NAKAMURA)
23 stitches x 34 rows

23 stitches x 20 rows

21 stitches x 20 rows

23 stitches x 20 rows

14 stitches x 28 rows

15 stitches x 30 rows

16 stitches x 31 rows

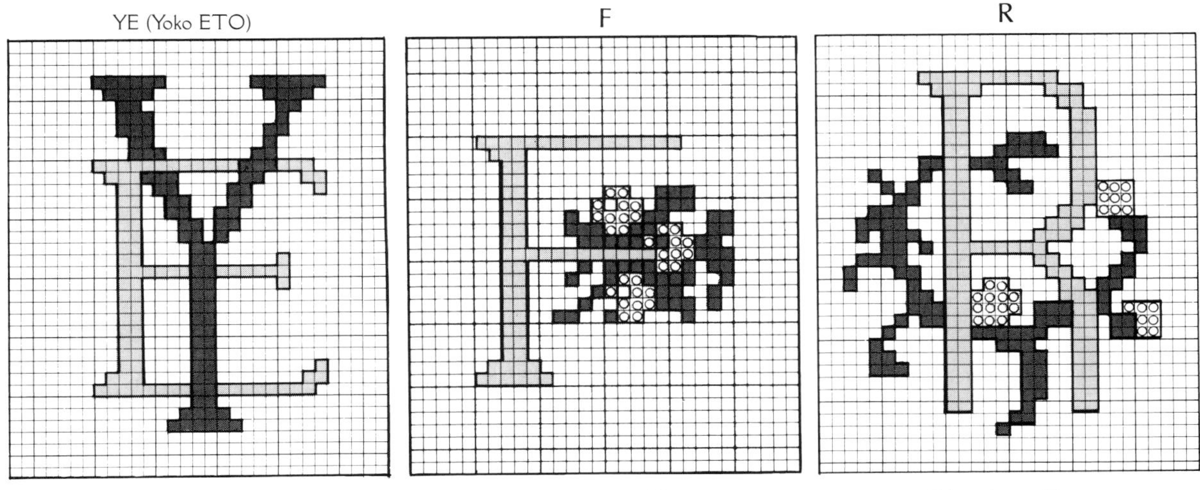

Small Articles

Pictured on page 21

A white brooch attached at the center of cloth ribbon.

A luxurious corsage with many petals.

A polka dotted pattern bow can be used to decorate the neck or used as a hair ornament.

A small panel decorates your favorite gloves.

Twin brooches in flower patterns used as a tieback for scarfs. Weave two panels and join them with twisted strands of beads.

A necklace made from a band with a slit provided in the middle.

Polka Dotted Bow

Finished size: 5cm x 18cm

● MATERIALS

Beads . . .Nickel (TB711) 10g, Black (TB49) 10g
Thread . . . . .Black
Supplies . . . . Metal finding
Horizontal & Vertical Rows . . . . .35 x 111

● PROCEDURE

The black polka dotted pattern is arranged on the nickel background. The opposite side is reversed and the top of ribbon is accented with a vertically-striped pattern.

At the center, reduce the number of stitches to shape the ribbon. Gather it with a silver metal fitting.

Combine two colors, a base color and a contrasting color, to simulate a reversible pattern.

Ribbon Decoration

Pictured on page 21

● MATERIALS

Beads . . . . .As listed
Thread . . . . .White
Ribbon . . . . .Black Velvet 5cm w x 28 cm lg
4 cm w x 28 cm lg
Horizontal & Vertical Rows . . . . .24 x 29

● PROCEDURE

Weave a triangle panel. Attach loops gradually making them larger toward the top.

How to gather

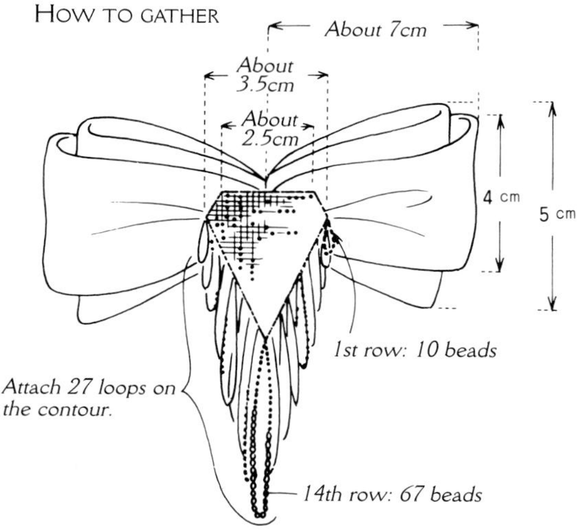

How to attach fringes

1st row	= 10 beads	8th row	= 34 beads
2nd row	= 13 beads	9th row	= 38 beads
3rd row	= 16 beads	10th row	= 42 beads
4th row	= 19 beads	11th row	= 46 beads
5th row	= 22 beads	12th row	= 51 beads
6th row	= 26 beads	13th row	= 58 beads
7th row	= 30 beads	14th row	= 67 beads

□ = White Aurora (TB161) 10g
● =. Green (TB707) 1g
× = Yellow Green (TB775) 1g
△ = Violet (TB771) 1g
▲ = Wine Red (TB332) 1g
○ = Yellow (TB903) 1g
■ = Blue (TB782) 1g

How to read the Stitch Chart

Figures in circles show the number of beads to be reduced. For example, item ③ shows that three 3 beads are reduced, so three 3 beads are not woven.

Row number									
1	③	18	③						
2	②	20	②						
3	①	22	①						
4	11	1●	2	2○	8				
5	10	3●	1	3○	7				
6	①	7	2●	1■	2●	3■	7	①	
7	①	7	2●	1■	3△	3■	6	①	
8	②	7	2△	1▲	2△	2■	2×	4	②
9	②	7	2△	3▲	2△	1×	5	②	
10	②	7	3△	2▲	2△	6	②		
11	③	5	2●	4△	1×	6	③		
12	③	6	1●	1■	1●	2△	1×	6	③
13	④	4	1●	1■	2●	2×	6	④	
14	④	3	1×	2●	1	1●	8	④	
15	④	5	1●	10	④				
16	⑤	14	⑤						
17	⑤	14	⑤						
18	⑥	12	⑥						
19	⑥	12	⑥						
20	⑦	10	⑦						
21	⑦	10	⑦						
22	⑧	8	⑧						
23	⑧	8	⑧						
24	⑨	6	⑨						
25	⑨	6	⑨						
26	⑩	4	⑩						
27	⑩	4	⑩						
28	⑪	2	⑪						
29	⑪	2	⑪						

Money Pouch *Pictured on page 23*

Finished size: 15.5cm x 21.5cm

● MATERIALS

Beads . . . . .Violet (TB771) 70g, Black (TB711), 50g, Frosted Black (TB610) 65g
Thread . . . . .Black
Lining . . . . .Black satin, 30cm x 40cm

● PROCEDURE

Pattern is beaded in light violet on a background of the frosted black beads, and fringed with glossy black beads.

The band is put through wide loops stitched on the face side.

For the loops weave 8 lines of 14 stitches x 48 rows, and locate as illustrated.

Make two beaded bands, 5m by 9 stitches, put them through the loops and stitch ends together in a loop.

Make an ornamental button in violet at the center section.

☒ = Black (TB49) 50g
◙ = Frosted Black (TB610) 65g
☐ = Violet (TB771) 70g

Silver Leaf Brooch

Pictured on page 23

Attach many beaded loops on the leaf panel to give it a dimensional appearance. Make a green drop with a glass on the leaf top end.

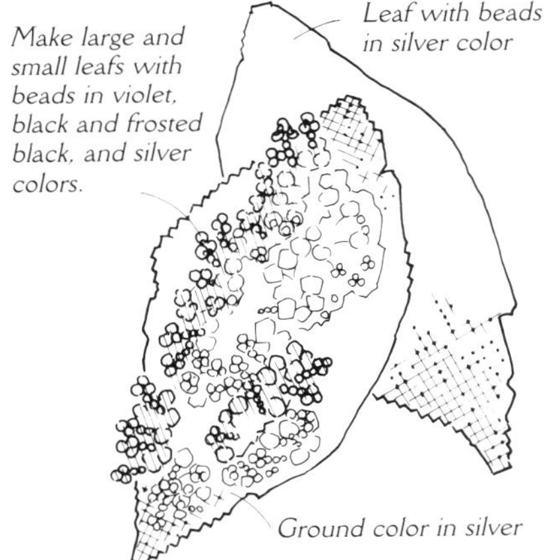

Overlap two leaves and fasten off.

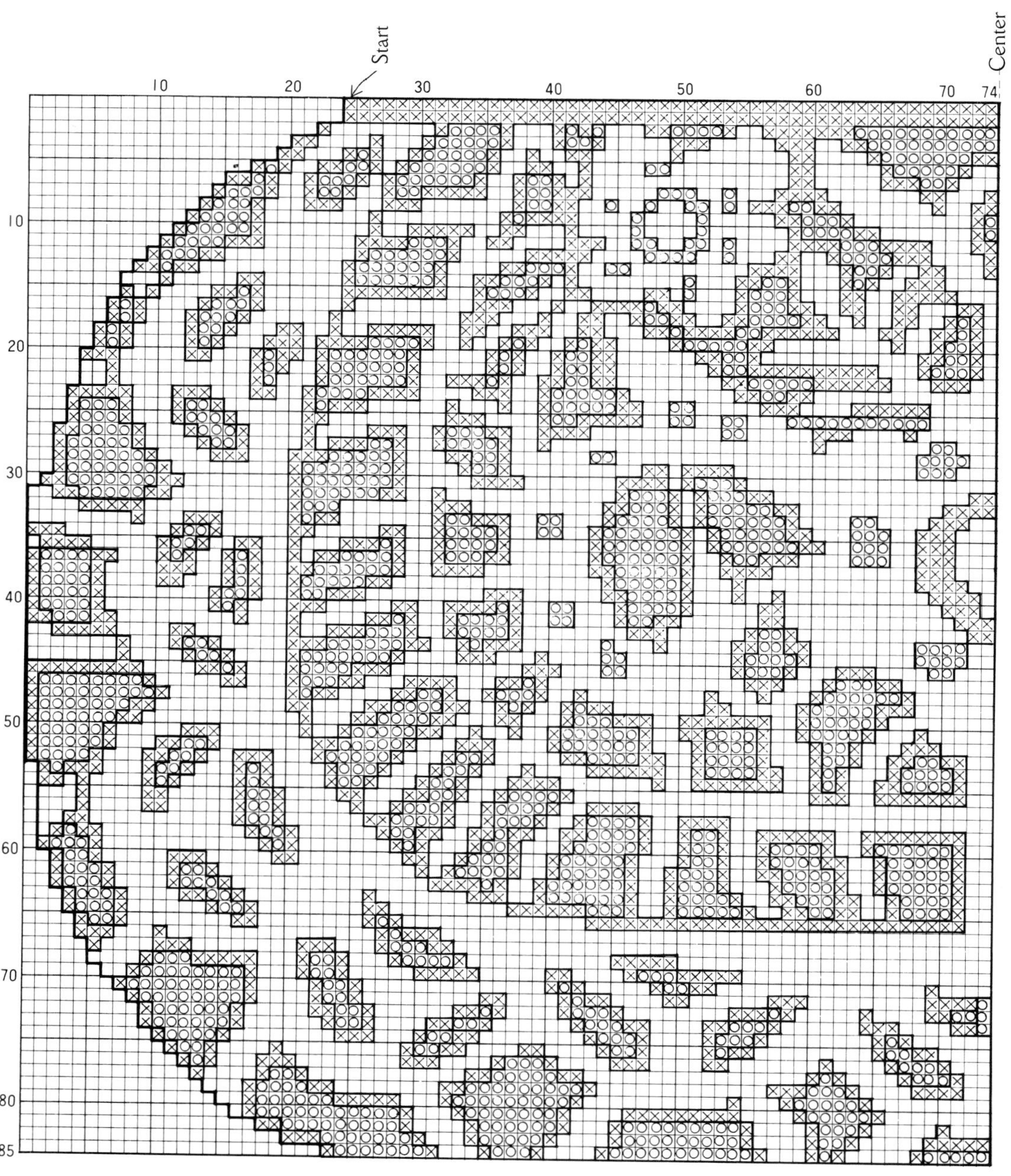
Start
Center
10
20
30
40
50
60
70
74
10
20
30
40
50
60
70
80
85

Rose Brooch

Pictured on page 22

Finished size: 11cm x 11cm

● MATERIALS

Beads . . . . .Violet (TB771) 30g, Nickel (TB711) 10g, Frosted Black (TB610) 10g
Thread . . . . .Gray
Supplies . . . . . . .Black felt 6cm x 4cm oval, Safety pin
Horizontal & Vertical Row: Flower . . . . . .18 x 50cm
Horizontal & Vertical Row: Bands 17 x 35cm, 2 panels

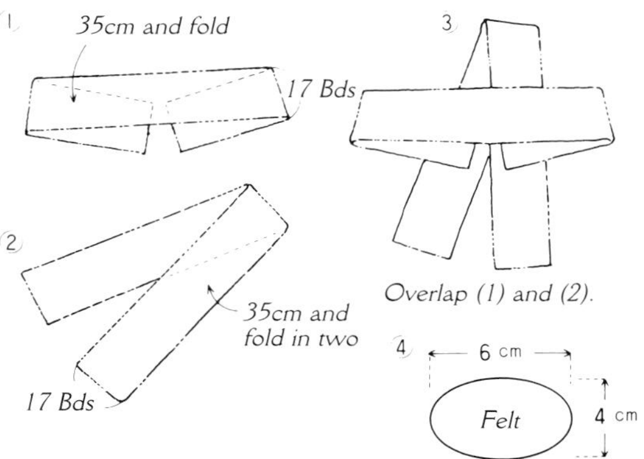

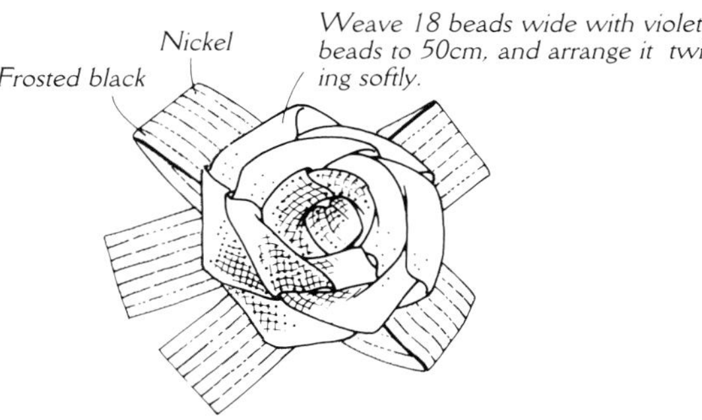

Stitch flowers on the panel, and sew the felt to it.

● PROCEDURE

Arrange the long panel woven with violet beads in a flower shape by softly twisting and coiling.
The texture gives the beautiful glass a look of velvet.
The leaf bands presents a sharp contrast with their frosted black and nickel vertically-striped beads. The two bands are woven with frosted black and nickel beads as 2, 3, 2, 3, 2, 3, 2.
Fold the bands in, and attach the flower on the panel front and attach a safety pin on the back to finish.

Total Fashion

Pictured on page 25

Pouch

The square bag is finished by folding the woven rectangular panel in two, sewing the sides and putting braid through. It is easy to make. Try it with a simple design.

Corsage

Finished size: 9cm x 10cm

● MATERIALS

Beads . . . . .Black (TB49) 3g, Silver (TB558) 6g, Nickel (TB711) 5g, Charcoal Gray (TB81) 5g
Thread . . . . .Black
Supplies . . . . .Corsage pin

● PROCEDURE

Make leaf panels in various colors, patterns and shapes (7 petals and 1 leaf). Arrange them as desired and attach corsage pin at the base to finish.

PETALS
2 black petals
2 charcoal gray petals
1 nickel petal
2 petals in checker pattern in 5 stitches x 5 rows
LEAF
1 leaf in checker pattern

Earring

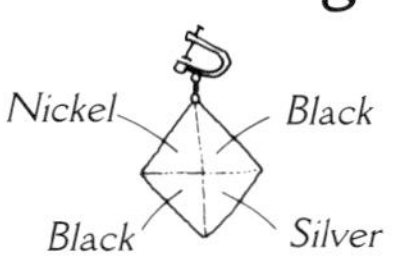

Bracelet

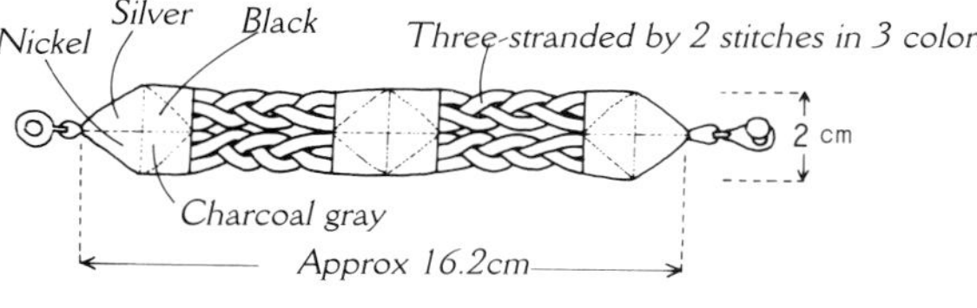

ACTUAL SIZE PATTERNS

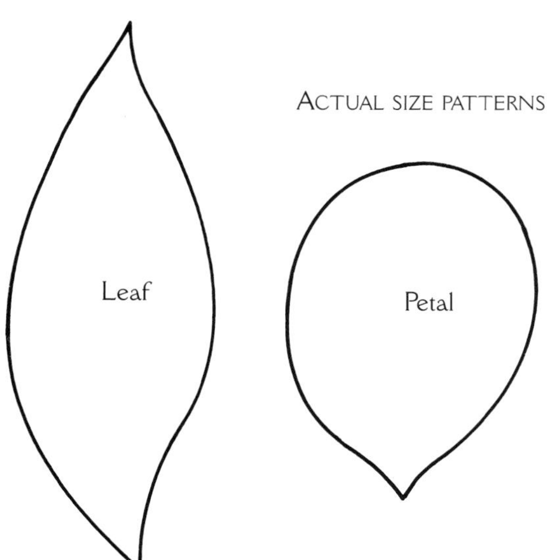

Venetian Glass

Pictured on page 26

Star Ribbon

Finished size: 4cm x 2.5cm

● MATERIALS

Beads . . . . .Silver 1g, Nickel 3g
Thread . . . . .Gray
Supplies .Satin beige ribbon, 3.5cm x 43cm,Safety pin
Horizontal & Vertical Row . . . . .18 x 18

● PROCEDURE

Weave two panels in star shape. Form ribbon as shown and sew the two stars on it. And attach a safety pin on the reverse side of the ribbon.

□ = Silver (TB21)
⊡ = Nickel (TB711)

Rows									
1	⑪	1	⑥						
2	⑩	2	⑥						
3	⑨	1	1●	1	⑥				
4	⑧	1	2●	1	⑥				
5		3	④	1	3●	1	⑥		
6		1	2●	3	①	1	3●	1	⑥
7	①	1	4●	1	4●	1	⑥		
8	②	1	9●	3	③				
9	③	1	11●	2	①				
10	③	1	13●	1					
11	③	1	12●	2					
12	②	1	10●	3	②				
13	①	1	9●	2	⑤				
14		1	2●	5	3●	1	⑥		
15		3	④	1	3●	1	⑥		
16	⑧	1	2●	1	⑥				
17	⑨	1	1●	1	⑥				
18	⑩	2	⑥						

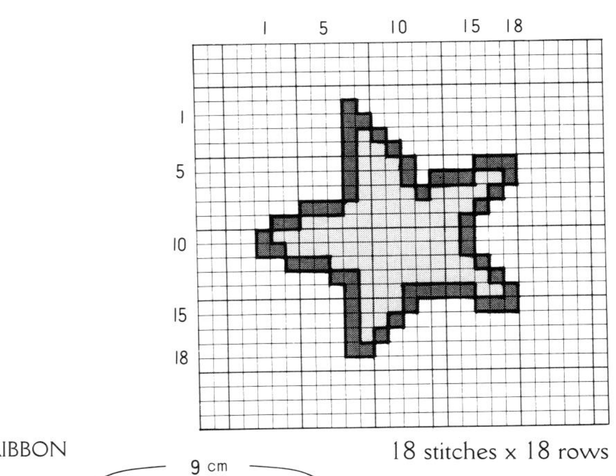

RIBBON

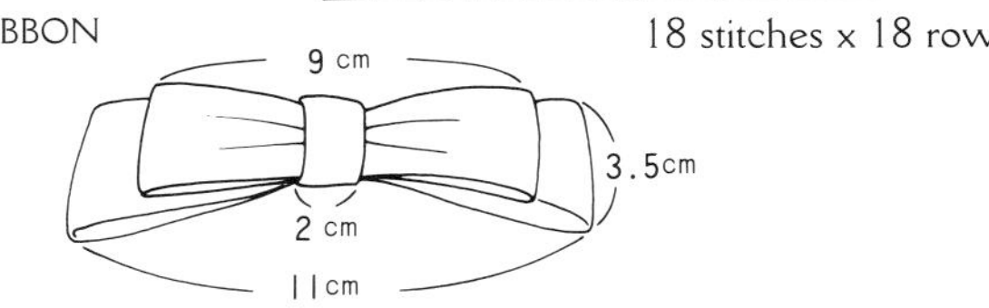

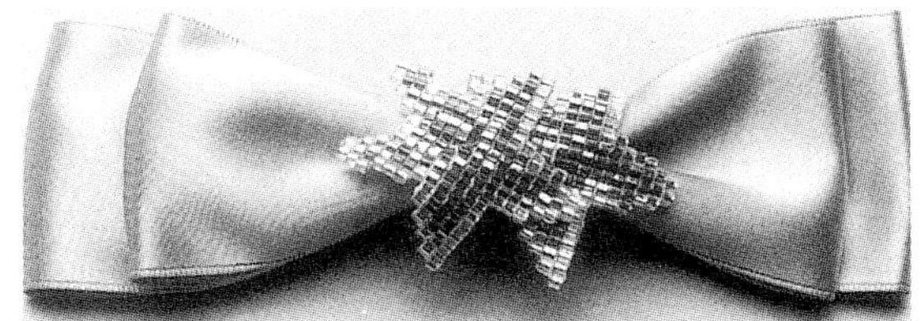

Chain Belt

pictured on page 27

Finished size: 3cm x Waist (about 65cm)

● MATERIALS

Beads . . . . .Nickel 10g, Silver 10g, White Aurora 10g
Thread . . . . .Gray
Supplies . . . . .Chain
Horizontal & Vertical Rows: Short Panel . . . . .21 x 54
Horizontal & Vertical Rows: Long Panel . . . .21 x 144

● PROCEDURE

The short panel is woven 21 stitches x 54 rows by repeating 1st to 18th row 3 times.

The long panel is woven 21 stitches x 144 rows by repeating 1st to 18th row 8 times.

Double all warp threads.

Finish off warps and attach the metal fittings. Put chains in the order of thick to fine.

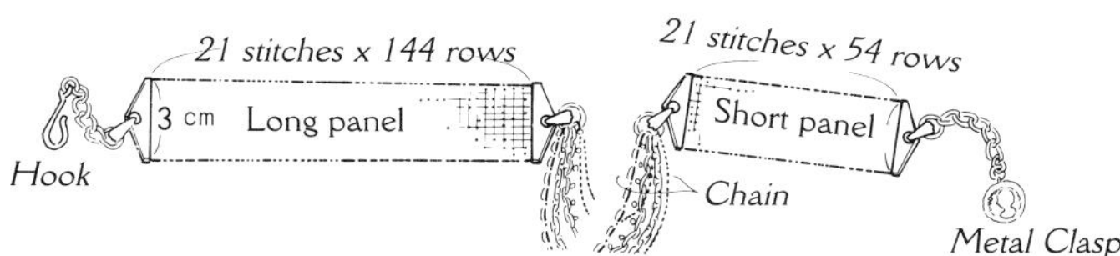

STITCH CHART FOR CHAIN BELT

1	1	1●	2	1●	2	1●	2	1●	2	1●	2	1●	2	1●	1		
2	1	1●	2	1●	2	1●	2	1●	2	1●	2	1●	2	1●	1		
3	1○	1	2○	1	2○	1	2○	1	2○	1	2○	1	2○	1	1○		
4	1	1●	2	1●	2	1●	2	1●	2	1●	2	1●	2	1●	1		
5	1	1●	2	1●	2	1●	2	1●	2	1●	2	1●	2	1●	1		
6	1○	1	2○	1	2○	1	2○	1	2○	1	2○	1	2○	1	1○		
7	1	1●	2	1●	2	1●	2	1●	2	1●	2	1●	2	1●	1		
8	1	1●	2	1●	2	1●	2	1●	2	1●	2	1●	2	1●	1		
9	1○	1	2○	1	2○	1	2○	1	2○	1	2○	1	2○	1	1○		
10	1	1●	2	1●	2	1●	2	1●	2	1●	2	1●	2	1●	1		
11	1	1●	2	1●	2	1●	2	1●	2	1●	2	1●	2	1●	1		
12	1○	1	2○	1	2○	1	2○	1	2○	1	2○	1	2○	1	1○		
13	1	1●	2	1●	2	1●	2	1●	2	1●	2	1●	2	1●	1		
14	1	1●	2	1●	2	1●	2	1●	2	1●	2	1●	2	1●	1		
15	1○	1	2○	1	2○	1	2○	1	2○	1	2○	1	2○	1	1○		
16	1	1●	2	1●	2	1●	2	1●	2	1●	2	1●	2	1●	1		
17	1	1●	2	1●	2	1●	2	1●	2	1●	2	1●	2	1●	1		
18	1○	1	2○	1	2○	1	2○	1	2○	1	2○	1	2○	1	1○		

□ = Silver (TB21)
● = White Aurora (TB161)
◎ = Nickel (TB711)

Paper Lantern Pendant

Pictured on page 28

Finished size: 2.5cm x 6.7cm

● MATERIALS

Beads . . . . Gold Mix (TB712 & TB22) 5g
Thread . . . . Gray
Supplies . . . . Chain, Styrofoam Ball
Horizontal & Vertical Rows . . . . 25 x 45

● PROCEDURE

Warp 25 threads and weave 45 rows increasing and decreasing the number of stitches according to the Stitch Chart.
After drawing the panel as illustrated, put the foam ball in the panel as a form. Stitch the side and attach 10 strands of fringe at the center.

STITCH CHART FOR PENDANT
Mix Gold (TB712 and TB22)

Row	Stitches	Row	Stitches
1	8	24	24
2	10	25	24
3	14	26	18
4	20	27	14
5	22	28	8
6	24	29	10
7	24	30	14
8	18	31	20
9	14	32	22
10	8	33	24
11	10	34	24
12	14	35	18
13	20	36	14
14	22	37	8
15	24	38	10
16	24	39	14
17	18	40	20
18	14	41	22
19	8	42	24
20	10	43	24
21	14	44	18
22	20	45	14
23	22		

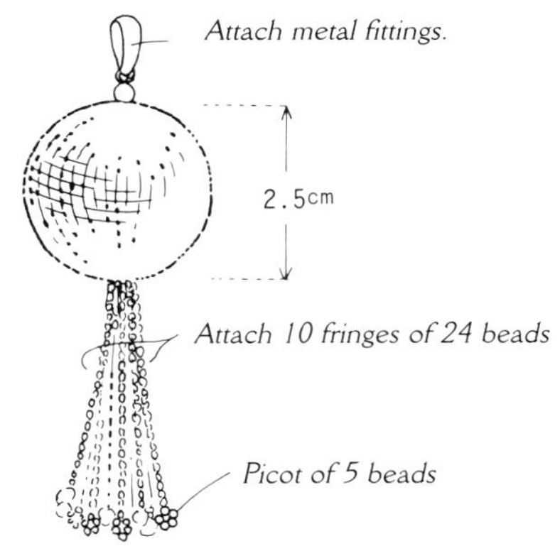

Tying off threads

As A Guest

Pictured on page 30

The silver handbag is ornamented with two rows of fringe following the slanting line.

The necklace obtains elegance by varying the length of beads at the center section where it becomes larger.

The belt, woven like a long band can be tied into a bow knot at the waist or it can be used as a necklace.

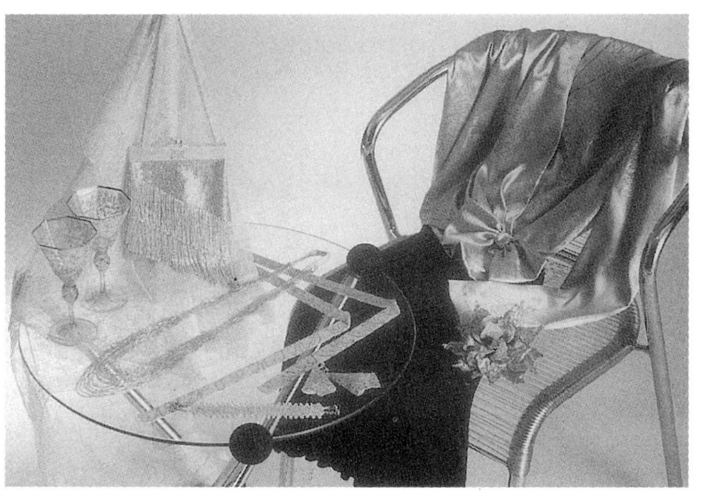

Bracelet

Finished size: 3cm x 16.2cm

● MATERIALS

Beads . . . . Silver (TB558) 6g, Silver (TB21) 6g
Thread . . . . .Beige
Supplies . . . . .Hook, 2 sets
Horizontal & Vertical Row . . . . .10 x 105

● PROCEDURE

Warp 11 threads, about 70cm. Silver (TB558) and Silver (TB21) beads are used in combination.
The warp is finished by attaching metal fittings. Since the width of the panel is wide, two metal fittings are suggested.
Make 5 bead picots around the woven panel as a decorative element.

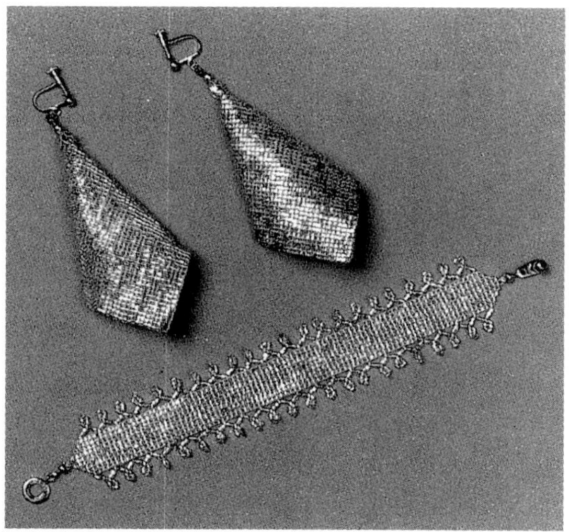

Earring

● PROCEDURE

Weave 2 panels of 37 stitches x 34 rows mixing Silver (TB558) and Silver (TB21) beads.
After finishing the warp, stitch the two sides together as shown and attach the metal fittings.

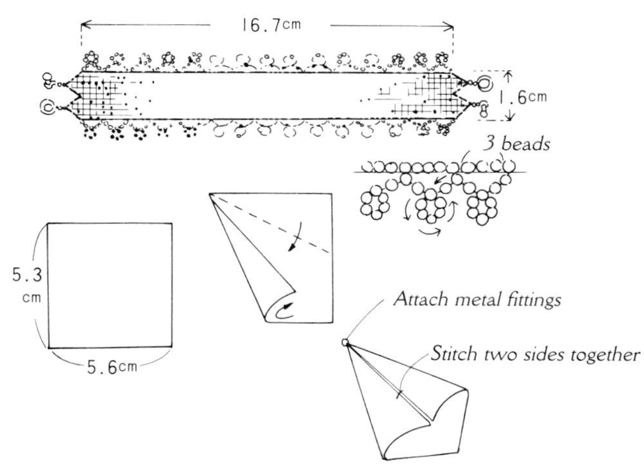

Paisley Brooch

Pictured on page 32

Finished size: 3cm x 9cm

The rhythmical paisley pattern in the form of *MAGATAMA* will provide feelings of pleasure. The paisley pattern, often used as a pattern in textile design, is suitable for both casual and formal environments by altering colors.

● MATERIALS

Beads . . . . Frosted Black (TB610) 2g, Frosted Green (TB710) 5g, Gold (TB712) 2g, Red Gold (TB503) 2g, Silver (TB558) 1g
Thread . . . . .Gray
Supplies . . . . .3cm Gold metal brooch pin
Horizontal & Vertical Row . . . . .21 x 56

STITCH CHART FOR
PETIT PAISLEY BROOCH

1	④		1		④						
2	③		1	1○	1		③				
3	②		1	3○	1		②				
4	①		1	1○	1●	3○	1		①		
5	1	1○	1●	5○	1						
6	1	1○	2●	4○	1						
7	1	1○	3●	3○	1						
8	1	1○	1●	2△	1●	2○	1				
9	1	1○	1●	1×	1△	1●	2○	1			
10	1	1○	1●	1△	1×	1△	1●	1○	1		
11	1	1○	1●	1△	1×	1△	1●	1○	1		
12	1	2○	1●	2△	1●	1○	1				
13	1	2○	1●	2△	1●	1○	1				
14	①		1	1○	3●	1○	1		①		
15	②		1	3○	1		②				
16	③		1	1○	1		③				
17	④		1		④						
18											

See page 112 for symbol key for beads.

Stitch Chart II for Paisley Brooch

- ☐ = Frosted Black (TB610)
- ◎ = Frosted Green (TB710)
- ☒ = Pure Gold (TB712)
- ● = Red Gold (TB503)
- △ = Silver (TB558)

1	21																	
2	1	5○	4×	10○	1													
3	1	3○	2×	4●	1×	3○	3×	3○	1									
4	1	2○	2×	2●	2△	1●	2×	1○	1×	3●	2×	1○	1					
5	1	1○	2×	2●	2△	2●	2×	1○	1×	4●	1×	1○	1					
6	1	1○	1×	2●	1△	3●	2×	2○	1×	1●	1△	2●	1×	1○	1			
7	1	1○	1×	6●	1×	3○	1×	1△	2●	2×	1○	1						
8	1	1○	1×	1●	1△	3●	2×	2○	1×	3●	2×	1○	1×	1				
9	1	1○	1×	1●	1△	3●	1×	3○	1×	2●	2×	1○	1×	1○	1			
10	1	1○	1×	2●	1△	1●	1×	4○	1×	1●	2×	2○	1×	1○	1			
11	1	1○	1×	4●	1×	4○	3×	2○	2×	1○	1							
12	1	1○	2×	2●	2×	3○	3×	3○	2×	1○	1							
13	1	2○	1×	2●	1×	4○	2×	3○	3×	1○	1							
14	1	2○	1×	2●	1×	3○	2×	4○	1×	1●	1×	1○	1					
15	1	3○	1×	1●	1×	2○	2×	4○	2×	1●	1×	1○	1					
16	1	3○	1×	1●	1×	1○	1×	6○	1×	2●	1×	1○	1					
17	1	4○	2×	7○	2×	2●	1×	1○	1									
18	1	2○	1●	2○	2×	5○	3×	2●	1×	1○	1							
19	1	1○	3●	3○	2×	2○	2×	4●	1×	1○	1							
20	1	2●	1△	2●	6○	1×	5●	1×	1○	1								
21	1	1●	3△	2●	4○	2×	2●	1△	1●	2×	1○	1						
22	1	1●	2△	1×	1△	1●	3○	2×	2●	1△	2●	1×	2○	1				
23	1	1●	1△	1×	2△	1●	2○	2×	6●	1×	2○	1						
24	1	1○	1●	2△	1●	2○	1×	5●	1△	2●	1×	2○	1					
25	1	1○	1●	1△	1●	2○	1×	4●	2△	3●	1×	2○	1					
26	1	2○	1●	2○	1×	4●	3△	2●	2×	2○	1							
27	1	2○	1●	1○	2×	9●	1×	3○	1									
28	1	1○	1●	2○	1×	4●	1△	4●	2×	3○	1							
29	1	1○	1●	2○	1×	3●	2△	4●	1×	4○	1							
30	①		1	3○	1×	2●	3△	3●	2×	3○	1		①					
31	②		1	2○	1×	2●	2△	3●	2×	3○	1		②					
32	③		1	1○	2×	6●	1×	3○	1		③							
33	④		1	1○	2×	2●	4×	2○	1		④							
34	⑤		1	1○	6×	2○	1		⑤									
35	⑥		1	7○	1		⑥											
36	⑦		1	5○	1		⑦											
37	⑧		1	3○	1		⑧											
38	⑨		1	1○	1		⑨											
39	⑩		1		⑩													
40																		

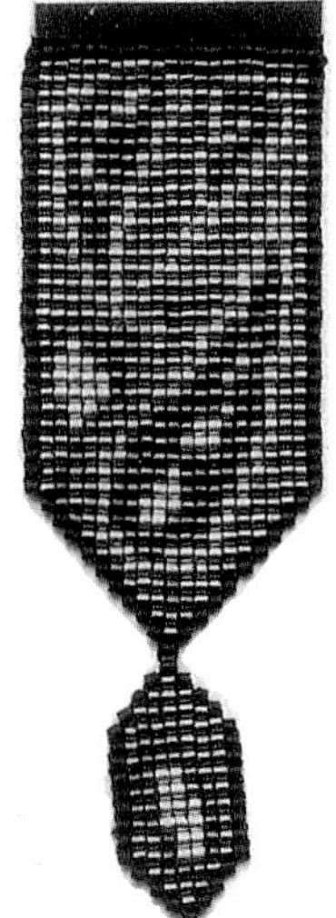

Designed For Autumn Brooch & Belt

Pictured on page 34

Finished size: Brooch 4.5cm x 7.5cm
Finished size: Belt 6cm x 72cm

This is an ensemble of pouch, brooch and belt on which initials are woven. The pouch is equipped with a fastener, and has a shape easy to cut and weave.

The brooch is in one pattern and the belt on which initials are designed is in a continuous sideway pattern. A metallic buckle compliments the design.

Ethnic Style Pouch

Pictured on page 33

Finished size: Pouch 18.7cm x 25cm
Small case: 11cm x 9.5cm

This is a money pouch and small article arranged in the Japanese style taking its inspiration from patterns of money pouches used several decades ago.

The small case can be used for a compact by providing it with a gusset which is woven separately. A fastener is attached inside. The pattern in soft colors is made striking by the vertical stripes.

Classic Party Bag & Bracelet

Pictured on page 36

Finished size:Bag 16.7cm x 24cm
Finished size:Bracelet 2.6cm x 16.2cm

Classical bag and bracelet in charcoal gray.

A stylish work on which a geometrical pattern is drawn in gold color. Part of the pattern is woven into the bracelet.

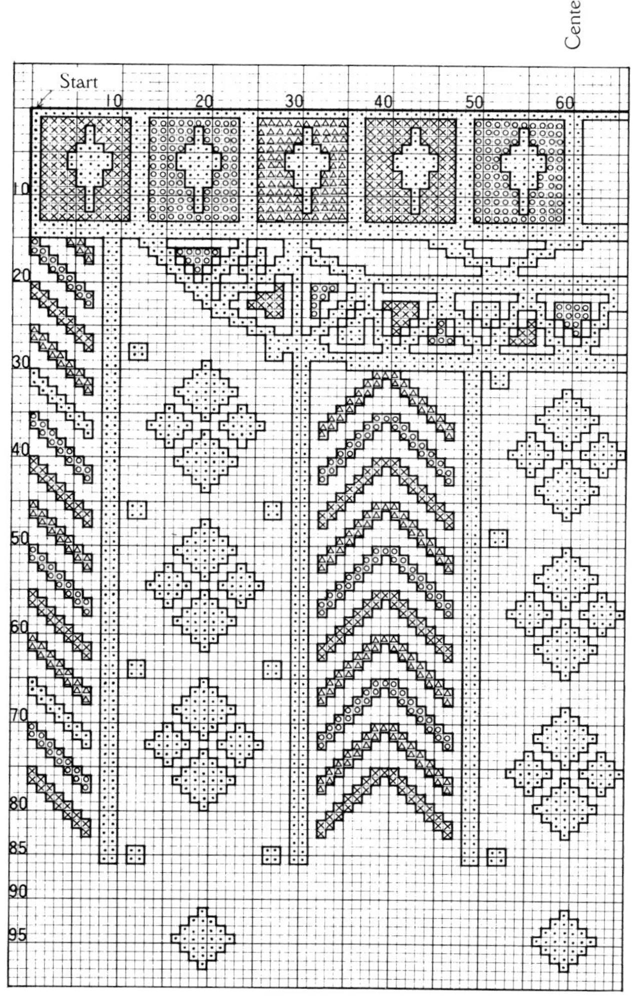

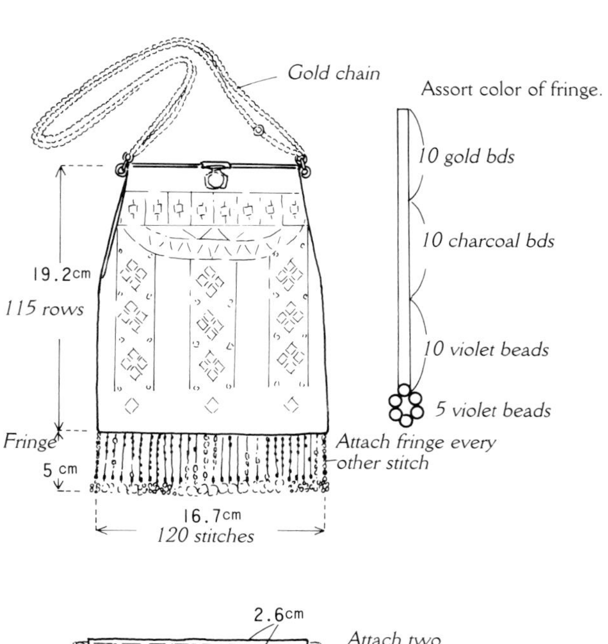

● MATERIALS

Beads . . . . .Listed below
Thread . . . . .Gray
Supplies . . . . .13cm Snap, Gold Chain
Lining . . . . .White satin 25cm x 60cm
Horizontal & Vertical Rows: Short Panel . . .120 x115

● PROCEDURE

This is a large bag suited to hold many things.

The fringe is attached to every other stitch from the panel.

Attach the metal fittings in order to have a secure hold on the panel. Take care that the panels on both ends do not sag.

□ = Charcoal Gray (TB81) 90g
● = Gold (TB712) 30g
× = Cobalt Blue (TB505) 10g
○ = Frosted Green (TB706) 15g
△ = Red (TB25) 15g

Stitch Chart I for Classical Party Bag

Rows																						
1	120																					
2	120																					
3	120																					
4	120																					
5	120																					
6	120																					
7	120																					
8	120																					
9	120																					
10	120●																					
11	1●	10×	2●	10○	2●	10△	2●	10×	2●	10○		2●										
12	1●	10×	2●	10○	2●	10△	2●	10×	2●	10○		2●										
13	1●	5×	1●	4×	2●	5○	1●	4○	2●	5△	1●	4△	2●	5×	1●	4×	2●	5○	1●	4○		2●
14	1●	5×	1●	4×	2●	5○	1●	4○	2●	5△	1●	4△	2●	5×	1●	4×	2●	5○	1●	4○		2●
15	1●	4×	3●	3×	2●	4○	3●	3○	2●	4△	3●	3△	2●	4×	3●	3×	2●	4○	3●	3○		2●
16	1●	3×	5●	2×	2●	3○	5●	2○	2●	3△	5●	2△	2●	3×	5●	2×	2●	3○	5●	2○		2●
17	1●	3×	5●	2×	2●	3○	5●	2○	2●	3△	5●	2△	2●	3×	5●	2×	2●	3○	5●	2○		2●
18	1●	4×	3●	3×	2●	4○	3●	3○	2●	4△	3●	3△	2●	4×	3●	3×	2●	4○	3●	3○		2●
19	1●	4×	3●	3×	2●	4○	3●	3○	2●	4△	3●	3△	2●	4×	3●	3×	2●	4○	3●	3○		2●
20	1●	5×	1●	4×	2●	5○	1●	4○	2●	5△	1●	4△	2●	5×	1●	4×	2●	5○	1●	4○		2●
21	1●	5×	1●	4×	2●	5○	1●	4○	2●	5△	1●	4△	2●	5×	1●	4×	2●	5○	1●	4○		2●
22	1●	5×	1●	4×	2●	5○	1●	4○	2●	5△	1●	4△	2●	5×	1●	4×	2●	5○	1●	4○		2●
23	1●	10×	2●	10○	2●	10△	2●	10×	2●	10○		2●										
24	120●																					
25	120●																					
26	1○	3	2△	2	2●	2	3●	8	1●	4	3●	13	4●	9		6●						
27	2○	3	2△	1	2●	3	3●	5○	1	2●	.1	1●	2	4●	14	3●	6	3●		4		

Advance stitches to the right end according to Stitch Chart and reverse weaving from the thick line leftward.

- ☐ = Charcoal Gray (TB81)
- ● = Gold (TB712)
- ☒ = Cobalt Blue (TB505)
- ○ = Frosted Green (TB706)
- △ = Red (TB25)

Stitch Chart II for Classical Party Bag

28	1	2○	3	1△	1	2●	4	2●	1	3○	1	2●	1	2●	1	3●	1	3●	14	3●	2	3●		8													
29	2	2○	4	2●	5	2●	1	1○	1	2●	1	2●	1	4●	3	4●	13	4●		12																	
30	3	2○	3	2●	6	2●	1	2●	3	3●	2	1●	5		50●																						
31	1×	3	2○	2	2●	7	3●	1	4●	2×	1○	1×	1	1×	3○	2	2●	1		42●																	
32	2×	3	2○	1	2●	8	2●	1	2●	2	3×	1	1●	1	2○	2	3●	7	2●	7	2●		8														
33	1	2×	3	1○	1	2●	9	3●	2	4×	1	1●	1	1○	2	2●	1	1●	1	4×	1	3●	2	3●	1	4●	1		4○								
34	2	2×	4	2●	10	3●	3	2×	1	1●	1	1○	1	2●	1	3●	1	3×	1●	4×	1	3●	1	1●	2	1●	1		4●								
35	3	2×	3	2●	12	3●	4	1●	2	2●	1	2●	1	1●	1	2×	1	2●	1○	1	2●	1	1●	1	2●	1	2●		1	2○	1						
36	1△	3	2×	2	2●	14	3●	2	1●	1	2●	1	3●	1	1●	1	1×	1	2●	1	1○	1	2●	2	2●	2	1×	1	1●		2	1○	1				
37	2△	3	2×	1	2●	16	6●	2	3●	1	2●	1	2●	1	3○	1	2●	1	2●	3×	1	2●		2													
38	1	2△	3	1×	1	2●	1	2●	13	2×	5●	6	3●	7	3●	6		4●																			
39	2	2△	4	2●	1	2●	13	2●	1	2●		58●																									
40	3	2△	3	2●	9	1●	9	2●	4	2×	5●	2×		32●																							
41	1●	3	2△	2	2●	8	3●	8	2●	7	3△	7	2●	1	2●		14																				
42	2●	3	2△	1	2●	7	5●	7	2●	6	2△	1	2△	6	2●	1	2●		14																		
43	1	2●	3	1△	1	2●	6	7●	6	2●	5	2△	3	2△	5	2●		9	1●	10																	
44	2	2●	4	2●	7	5●	7	2●	4	2△	5	2△	4	2●		8	3●	9																			
45	3	2●	3	2●	5	1●	2	3●	2	1●	5	2●	3	2△	7	2△	3	2●		7	5●	8															
46	1○	3	2●	2	2●	4	3●	2	1●	2	3●	4	2●	2	2△	3	3○	3	2△	2	2●		6	7●	7												
47	2○	3	2●	1	2●	3	5●	3	5●	3	2●	1	2△	3	2○	1	2○	3	2△	1	2●		7	5●	8												
48	1	2○	3	1●	1	2●	4	3●	2	1●	2	3●	4	2●	1	1△	3	2○	3	2○	3	1△	1	2●		5	1●	2	3●	2	1●	6					
49	2	2○	4	2●	5	1●	2	3●	2	1●	5	2●	4	2○	5	2○	4	2●		4	3●	2	1●	2	3●	5											
50	3	2○	3	2●	7	5●	7	2●	3	2○	7	2○	3	2●		3	5●	3	5●	4																	
51	1×	3	2○	2	2●	6	7●	6	2●	2	2○	3	3×	3	2○	2	2●		4	3●	2	1●	2	3●	5												
52	2×	3	2○	1	2●	7	5●	7	2●	1	2○	3	2×	1	2×	3	2○	1	2●		5	1●	2	3●	2	1●	6										
53	1	2×	3	1○	1	2●	8	3●	8	2●	1	1○	3	2×	3	2×	3	1○	1	2●		7	5●	8													
54	2	2×	4	2●	9	1●	9	2●	4	2×	5	2×	4	2●		6		7●	7																		
55	3	2×	3	2●	19	2●	3	2×	7	2×	3	2●		7	5●	8																					
56	1△	3	2×	2	2●	1	2●	13	2●	1	2●	2	2×	3	3△	3	2×	2	2●		8		3●	9													
57	2△	3	2×	1	2●	1	2●	13	2●	1	2●	1	2×	3	2△	1	2△	3	2×	1	2●		9		1●	10											
58	1	2△	3	1×	1	2●	9	1●	9	2●	1	1×	3	2△	3	2△	3	1×	1	2●		20															
59	2	2△	4	2●	8	3●	8	2●	4	2△	5	2△	4	2●	1	2●		14																			
60	3	2△	3	2●	7	5●	7	2●	3	2△	7	2△	3	2●	1	2●		14																			
61	1○	3	2△	2	2●	6	7●	6	2●	2	2△	3	3○	3	2△	2	2●		9	1●	10																
62	2○	3	2△	1	2●	7	5●	7	2●	1	2△	3	2○	1	2○	3	2△	1	2●		8	3●	9														
63	1	2○	3	1△	1	2●	5	1●	2	3●	2	1●	5	2●	1	1△	3	2○	3	2○	3	1△	1	2●		7		5●	8								
64	2	2○	4	2●	4	3●	2	1●	2	3●	4	2●	4	2○	5	2○	4	2●		6	7●	7															
65	3	2○	3	2●	3	5●	3	5●	3	2●	3	2○	7	2○	3	2●		7	5●	8																	
66	1×	3	2○	2	2●	4	3●	2	1●	2	3●	4	2●	2	2○	3	3×	3	2○	2	2●		5	1●	2	3●	2	1●	6								
67	2×	3	2○	1	2●	5	1●	2	3●	2	1●	5	2●	1	2○	3	2×	1	2×	3	2○	1	2●		4	3●	2	1●	2	3●	5						
68	1	2×	3	1○	1	2●	7	5●	7	2●	1	1○	3	2×	3	2×	3	1○	1	2●		3	5●	3	5●	4											
69	2	2×	4	2●	6	7●	6	2●	4	2×	5	2×	4	2●		4	3●	2	1●	2	3●	5															
70	3	2×	3	2●	7	5●	7	2●	3	2×	7	2×	3	2●		5	1●	2	3●	2	1●	6															
71	1△	3	2×	2	2●	8	3●	8	2●	2	2×	3	3△	3	2×	2	2●		7	5●	8																

□ = Charcoal Gray (TB81)
● = Gold (TB712)
× = Cobalt Blue (TB505)
○ = Frosted Green (TB706)
△ = Red (TB25)

STITCH CHART III FOR CLASSICAL PARTY BAG

Row	Stitches (to thick line)	Stitches (after thick line)
72	2△ 3 2× 1 2● 9 1● 9 2● 1 2× 3 2△ 1 2△ 3 2× 1 2●	6 7● 7
73	1 2△ 3 1× 1 2● 19 2● 1 1× 3 2△ 3 2△ 3 1× 1 2●	7 5● 8
74	2 2△ 4 2● 1 2● 13 2● 1 2● 4 2△ 5 2△ 4 2●	8 3● 9
75	3 2△ 3 2● 1 2● 13 2● 1 2● 3 2△ 7 2△ 3 2●	9 1● 10
76	1● 3 2△ 2 2● 9 1● 9 2● 2 2△ 3 3○ 3 2△ 2 2●	20
77	2● 3 2△ 1 2● 8 3● 8 2● 1 2△ 3 2○ 1 2○ 3 2△ 1 2● 1 2●	14
78	1 2● 3 1△ 1 2● 7 5● 7 2● 1 1△ 3 2○ 3 2○ 3 1△ 1 2● 1 2●	14
79	2 2● 4 2● 6 7● 6 2● 4 2○ 5 2○ 4 2●	9 1● 10
80	3 2● 3 2● 7 5● 7 2● 3 2○ 7 2○ 3 2●	8 3● 9
81	1○ 3 2● 2 2● 5 1● 2 3● 2 1● 5 2● 2 2○ 3 3△ 3 2○ 2 2●	7 5● 8
82	2○ 3 2● 1 2● 4 3● 2 1● 2 3● 4 2● 1 2○ 3 2△ 1 2△ 3 2○ 1 2●	6 7● 7
83	1 2○ 3 1● 1 2● 3 5● 3 5● 3 2● 1 1○ 3 2△ 3 2△ 3 1○ 1 2●	7 5● 8
84	2 2○ 4 2● 4 3● 2 1● 2 3● 4 2● 4 2△ 5 2△ 4 2●	5 1● 2 3● 2 1● 6
85	3 2○ 3 2● 5 1● 2 3● 2 1● 5 2● 3 2△ 7 2△ 3 2●	4 3● 2 1● 2 3● 5
86	1× 3 2○ 2 2● 7 5● 7 2● 2 2△ 3 3× 3 2△ 2 2●	3 5● 3 5● 4
87	2× 3 2○ 1 2● 6 7○ 6 2● 1 2△ 3 2× 1 2× 3 2△ 1 2●	4 3● 2 1● 2 3● 5
88	1 2× 3 1○ 1 2● 7 5● 7 2● 1 1△ 3 2× 3 2× 3 1△ 1 2●	5 1● 2 3● 2 1● 6
89	2 2× 4 2● 8 3● 8 2● 4 2× 5 2× 4 2●	7 5● 8
90	3 2× 3 2● 9 1● 9 2● 3 2× 7 2× 3 2●	6 7● 7
91	4 2× 2 2● 19 2● 2 2× 9 2× 2 2●	7 5● 8
92	5 2× 1 2● 19 2● 1 2× 11 2× 1 2●	8 3● 9
93	6 1× 1 2● 19 2● 1 1× 13 1× 1 2●	9 1● 10
94	8 2● 19 2● 17 2●	20
95	8 2● 1 2● 13 2● 1 2● 17 2● 1 2●	14
96	8 2● 1 2● 13 2● 1 2● 17 2● 1 2●	14
97	120	
98	120	
99	120	
100	120	
101	19 1●	39 1● 40
102	18 3●	37 3● 38
103	17 5●	35 5● 36
104	16 7●	33 7● 34
105	17 5●	35 5● 36
106	18 3●	37 3● 38
107	19 1●	39 1● 40
108	120	
109	120	
110	120	
111	120	
112	120	
113	120	
114	120	
115	120	

Advance stitches to the right end according to STITCH CHART and reverse weaving from the thick line leftward.

Evening Glow Handbag

Pictured on page 39

Finished size: 12.5cm x 21cm

● MATERIALS

Beads . . . .Dark Brown 50g, Wine Red 70g, Red Gold 50g
Thread . . . . .Red
Supplies . . . . .Snap
Lining . . . . .Red satin 30cm x 40cm
Horizontal & Vertical Rows: Short Panel . . . .148 x 84

● PROCEDURE

Weave the bottom of handbag forming a curve. Attach a 17 cm snap.

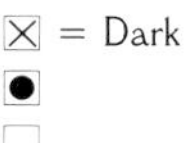

× = Dark

STITCH CHART I FOR HANDBAG

1		148×												
2		148×												
3	22●	1×	8●	1×	4	1×	3●	1×	3	3●	2×	4	1×	2●
4	20●	2×	4●	1×	3●	1×	5	1×	3●	1×	2	1×	5●	1×
5	19●	2×	3●	1×	1	1×	2●	1×	5	1×	2●	1×	2●	2×
6	17●	1×	1	1×	2●	1×	3	1×	1●	1×	6	1×	2●	2×
7	15●	1×	2	1×	2●	1×	3	1×	1●	1×	6	1×	2●	1×
8	14●	1×	3	1×	2●	1×	2	1×	2●	1×	2	5×	2●	1×
9	13●	1×	3	1×	3●	3×	3●	3×	7●	1×	2	2×	2●	1
10	12●	1×	4	1×	8●	1×	9●	1×	1	4×	4●	1	4●	1
11	11●	1×	5	1×	8●	1×	2●	5×	2●	2×	3●	1×	4●	1
12	10●	1×	4	3×	7●	4×	3	1×	2●	2×	4●	3×	2●	2
13	9●	1×	3	2×	10●	1×	6	1×	5●	5×	4●	4	2●	1
14	8●	2×	1	2×	11●	1×	6	1×	4●	2×	3	1×	2●	2
15	10●	1×	5●	2×	6●	1×	6	1×	2●	2×	3	1×	1●	1×
16	7●	1×	1●	1×	4●	2×	1	1×	6●	8×	2●	1×	3	1×
17	6●	1×	1	1×	4●	1×	3	1×	6●	1×	9●	3×	3●	1×
18	6●	1×	1	1×	3●	1×	3	1×	6●	1×	9●	3×	3●	1×
19	5●	1×	1	1×	4●	1×	2	1×	3●	2×	2●	1×	2●	5×
20	5●	1×	1	1×	4●	1×	1	1×	3●	1×	1	1×	1●	4×
21	4●	3×	5●	2×	3●	1×	1	1×	2●	1×	6	1×	5●	1×
22	6●	1×	10●	1×	1	1×	2●	1×	6	1×	5●	1×	1	1×
23	6●	1×	10●	1×	1	3●	1×	6	1×	2●	3×	1	1×	2●
24	3●	5×	3●	3×	3●	2×	2●	1×	4	4×	4●	3×	2●	1×
25	3●	1×	3	1×	3●	1×	2	1×	6●	1×	1	3×	6●	1×
26	3●	1×	3	1×	3●	1×	3	1×	5●	2×	9●	3×	4●	1×
27	2●	2×	4	1×	3●	1×	3	1×	4●	1×	4●	3×	2●	1×
28	2●	1×	5	1×	4●	1×	2	1×	4●	1×	1●	3×	2	1×
29	2●	1×	6	1×	4●	3×	3●	3×	5	1×	3●	2×	2	1×
30	2●	1×	7	1×	9●	1×	7	1×	4●	1×	2	1×	10●	2×
31	1●	2×	7	2×	8●	1×	7	1×	5●	4×	7●	4×	1●	1×
32	2●	2×	5	2×	9●	1×	6	2×	2●	1×	13●	1×	3	1×
33	4●	5×	11●	1×	3	3×	4●	3×	10●	2×	3	1×	1●	1×
34	8●	1×	3●	3×	5●	1×	1	2×	7●	1×	2	3×	2●	2
35	3×	8●	1×	2	1×	5●	2×	5●	2×	2●	1×	4	1×	2●
36	1●	4×	5●	1×	2	1×	2●	2×	2●	1×	3●	3×	1	1×
37	1×	4●	2×	3●	1×	2	2●	1×	1	1×	2●	1×	1●	2×
38	1×	4	1×	4●	1×	1	1×	2●	1×	1	1×	2●	2×	6
39	1×	4	1×	4●	2×	3●	1×	1	1×	2●	1×	5	2×	16●
40	1×	4	1×	8●	1×	2	1×	2●	1×	2	3×	9●	3×	6●
41	1×	4	1×	8●	1×	1	1×	3●	3×	5●	2×	2●	4×	1
42	2●	3	2×	9●	1×	3●	1×	5●	2×	1	1×	2●	1×	4

Advance stitches to the right end according to STITCH CHART and reverse weaving from the thick line leftward.

7×	11
1	1×	5●	3×	2●	2×	10
6●	1×	8●	2×	4●	1×	7	2×
2●	1×	4●	2	9●	2×	5●	1×	5	1×	2●
2	1×	1●	1×	15●	2×	5●	3×	2	1×	3●
2	3×	5●	3	2●	1	3●	4×	7●	2×	3●	1×
2●	1	2●	2	1●	1	1●	3×	2	2×	7●	1×	2●	2×
5●	2×	3	1×	9●	1×	1
4●	1	6●	1×	4	2×	7●	1×	1
2●	2	1●	1	4●	4×	3	4×	3●	2×
3●	2×	2●	1×	4	3×	4●	1×
9●	4×	3●	1×	2	1×	2●	2×	3●	1×
8●	1	3●	2×	2	1×	3●	1×	1	1×	2●	3×	4●
2●	2×	4●	2×	1●	1	3●	1×	3	1×	3●	2×	2●	5×	3●
2●	4×	1	2×	4●	1×	3	2×	2●	2×	2●	2×	3●	2×	1●
2●	2×	2●	1×	2	2×	2●	2×	4	2×	2●	1×	2●	2×	2●	1×	1	1×	1●
2●	2×	2●	3×	2●	2×	3●	2×	1	4×	2	6×	3●	2×	2●	2×	1	1×	1●
4	1×	2●	1×	2●	1×	1	1×	2●	1×	1	2×	4●	1×	5	2×	9●	1×	2●	1×	2	1×	1●
1	1×	2●	1×	2	2×	6●	2×	2	1×	12●	2×	2	1×	1●
2●	1×	2	2×	7●	1×	2	10×	3●	1×	3	1×	1●
2×	2	2×	8●	2×	5	6×	3●	3×	2●
5	1×	8●	2×	2	2×	14●
3●	1×	2●	1×	5	2×	2●	2	5●	3×	4●	6×	5●
2	5×	2●	2	2●	2	3●	11	5●
3	2×	2●	4×	10●	2	5●	3×	4●	1×	6●
2●	1×	4	1×	2●	1×	20●	1×	8●	2	3●
6●	2	23●	4	2●
1●	4×	14●	3	3●
3	1×	19●
1●	1×	3	2×	15●	2×
5	2×	11●	4×
3●	1×	4	1×	1●	1×	6	1×	4●	2	4●	3×	2●
2	2●	2×	5	1×	1●	1×	5	2×	3●	3	2●	3×	3●
2●	1×	4	1×	6●	1×	6	1×	1●	1×	6	2×	2●	3	2●	3×	3●
4	1×	2●	1×	3	2×	6●	1×	6	1×	2●	1×	2	3×	4●	3	2●	3×	3●
1×	2●	4×	8●	2×	5	1×	2●	4×	11●	3×	3●
1×	5	1×	3●	1×	13●	4×	2●
2×	4	1×	3●	1×	2●	1×	11●	4×	1●
1×	2●	2	3●	1×	4	1×	5●	2×	12●	3×	1●
1×	2●	2	3●	1×	2	2×	6●	2×	13●	3×

STITCH CHART II FOR HANDBAG

43	2●	5×	4●	2×	7●	1×	2●	3×	3	1×	2●	1×	4	1×	
44	7●	1×	3●	1×	2	1×	5●	3×	6	2×	2●	1×	1	3×	
45	7●	1×	4●	1×	2	1×	4●	1×	7	1×	4●	3×	3●	1×	
46	9×	4●	2×	1	1×	3●	1×	4	3×	10●	3×	3●	2	8●	
47	1×	8	1×	5●	2×	3●	1×	3	2×	3●	4×	3●	2×	1	
48	1×	9	1×	9●	1×	1	2×	4●	2×	2	1×	2●	1×	3	
49	1×	7	2×	10●	2×	4●	2×	4	2×	2●	1×	1	1×	2●	
50	1×	6	2×	12●	1×	3●	2×	4	2×	3●	2×	3●	1×	3	
51	1×	5	1×	5●	3×	6●	1×	2●	1×	5	2×	2●	1×	2●	
52	1×	5	1×	3●	2×	2	1×	7●	2×	5	1×	3●	3×	4●	
53	①	1×	1	3×	3●	1×	2	1×	3●	1×	1	1×	4●	1×	
54	①	5×	3●	4×	3●	3×	4●	1×	3●	1×	3●	1×	2●	1×	
55	①	4×	4●	3×	4●	3×	4●	4×	3●	4×	3●	4×	7●	1×	
56	①	3●	1×	4●	2×	5●	1×	2	1×	4●	2×	3●	2×	2	
57	①	3●	1×	4●	2×	5●	1×	2	1×	5●	2×	1●	1×	3	
58	①	2●	2×	11●	1×	2	1×	6●	2×	4	1×	2●	1×	3	
59	①	1●	1×	1	2×	11●	1×	2	1×	6●	1×	2	2×	2●	
60	①	1×	3	1×	12●	1×	1	1×	7●	3×	3	1×	2●	1×	
61	②	1×	2	1×	5●	3×	5●	2×	8●	2×	2●	1×	3	1×	
62	②	1×	3	1×	4●	1×	2	1×	15●	1×	1●	1×	4	1×	
63	②	1×	3	1×	4●	1×	3	1×	15●	4×	1	1×	2●	1×	
64	③	1×	3	1×	4●	2×	2	1×	9●	1×	7●	3×	2●	1×	
65	③	1×	3	1×	6●	1×	2	1×	8●	2×	9●	6×	3	1×	
66	④	1×	2	1×	8●	2×	8●	1×	1	1×	14●	29×	2●		
67	④	3×	3●	1×	16●	1×	1	3×	42●						
68	⑤	1×	4●	3×	8●	3×	3●	1×	3	2×	41●				
69	⑤	1×	3●	1×	3	5×	3●	1×	2	1×	3●	1×	4	1×	
70	⑥	1×	2●	1×	7	1×	3●	1×	2	1×	5●	5×	5●	2×	
71	⑦	1×	9	1×	4●	1×	2	1×	14●	1×	1	1×	5●	1×	
72	⑧	1×	8	1×	4●	1×	2	1×	9●	2×	4●	1×	1	2×	
73	⑨	1×	6	1×	5●	2×	2	1×	6●	2×	1	1×	4●	1×	
74	⑨	1×	6	1×	6●	1×	2	1×	4●	2×	2	1×	6●	1×	
75	⑩	1×	4	1×	8●	3×	3●	1×	2	2×	8●	1×	3	1×	
76	⑪	1×	2	1×	4●	1×	9●	1×	2	2×	4●	2×	4●	1×	
77	⑫	1×	1	1×	3●	3×	8●	3×	4●	2×	2	1×	4●	3×	
78	⑬	1×	4●	1×	2	1×	12●	2×	5	2×	17●	1×	1	1×	
79	⑭	3●	1×	4	2×	8●	2×	9	1×	13●	3×	3	1×	4●	
80	⑮	2●	1×	6	5×	3●	1×	9	1×	11●	1×	3●	1×	5	
81	⑯	1●	1×	11	1×	3●	1×	7	1×	4●	9×	4●	1×	5	
82	⑱	2×	9	1×	4●	1×	6	1×	3●	1×	9	1×	4●	1×	
83	⑳	3×	7	1×	3●	1×	5	1×	4●	1×	9	1×	4●	1×	
84	㉓	1×	7	1×	3●	1×	3	1×	4●	1×	11	1×	3●	1×	

Advance stitches to the right end according to STITCH CHART and reverse weaving from the thick line leftward.

8●	3×	6●	1×	2	1×	13●	2×																							
6●	1	3●	1×	5●	2×	2	2×	8●	4	2●																				
4●	2	8●	1×	4	1×	8●	4	2●																						
1×	3	1×	3●	3×	4●	2	3●																							
1×	15●	3×	3●	1×	3	2×	7●																							
1×	2●	1×	9●	1×	3●	1×	3●	1×	6	1×	6●																			
1×	1	2×	7●	2×	5●	1×	5	3×	6●																					
3×	2●	7×	2●	1×	5	1×	8●																							
1×	2●	1×	6	1×	2●	2×	4	1×	2●	1×	4	1×	3●	1×	5●															
1×	6	1×	3●	1×	4	1×	3●	1×	2	1×	3●	3×	4●																	
3	1×	3●	1×	2	1×	3●	1×	4●	6×	2●	1×	4	2×	2●	1×	2●	1	3●	1×	4	1×	2●								
3●	1×	4●	6×	2●	1×	4●	2	2●	1×	1●	1×	3●	1×	4	1×	2●														
2●	7×	2●	1×	1	1×	2●	2×	4	1×	2●																				
1×	2●	1×	4	1×	18●	3×	2●	7×	2●																					
1×	2●	1×	4	1×	2●	4×	27●																							
1×	2●	1×	4	1×	2●	4×	20●																							
2×	1	2×	2●	2×	4	1×	2●	1×	2	1×	2●	6×	2●	8×	2●															
3●	1×	5	1×	2●	1×	2	1×	2●	1×	4	1×	2●	1×	6	1×	2●														
2●	1×	5	1×	3●	1×	2	1×	2●	1×	4	2×	2●	1×	5	1×	2●														
2●	1×	5	1×	2●	1×	3	1×	2●	2×	4	1×	2●	1×	5	1×	2●														
6	1×	2●	1×	3	1×	3●	1×	4	1×	2●	1×	5	1×	2●																
6	1×	2●	1×	4	1×	2●	2×	3	2×	2●	1×	4	1×	2●																
2●	1×	5	1×	2●	2×	2	2×	2●	1×	4	1×	2●																		
11●	5×	24●																												
4●	1×	3	5×	19●																										
2	2×	16●	1×	4●																										
4●	2×	6●	3×	9●	4×	1																								
3	1×	8●	3×	1	1×	5●	1×	4●	2×	3																				
3	2×	4●	2×	3	1×	6●	3×	4●	2×	1																				
4●	1×	3	1×	8●	1×	1	1×	6●																						
2	1×	4●	1×	1	2×	9●	1×	2	2×	4●																				
4●	2×	7●	1×	4●	1×	3	1×	3●																						
4●	1×	3	1×	2●																										
4×	2●																													
1×	9●																													
1×	8●																													
3	1×	5●	1×	3●																										
2	1×	5●	5×																											
1	1×	5●	1×	5																										

Lavender

Pictured on page 40

Finished size: Brooch 5.4cm x 12.4cm
Finished size: Handbag 16.2cm x 26.5cm
Finished size: Belt 5.5cm x 65cm

Bag and belt are made from the same pattern repeated continuously. By combining in different ways, one design can be developed into a variety of patterns.

It is a challenge to weave the three twisted braided section, but the reward will be the pleasure after completion.

- MATERIALS [Brooch]

Beads . . . . .Nickel (TB711) 6g, Dark Blue (TB82) 4g, Pink (TB145) 2g, Gold (TB712) 1g, Silver (TB714) 4g
Thread . . . . .Gray
Supplies .Brooch finding Snap
Horizontal & Vertical Rows . . . . .37 x 45

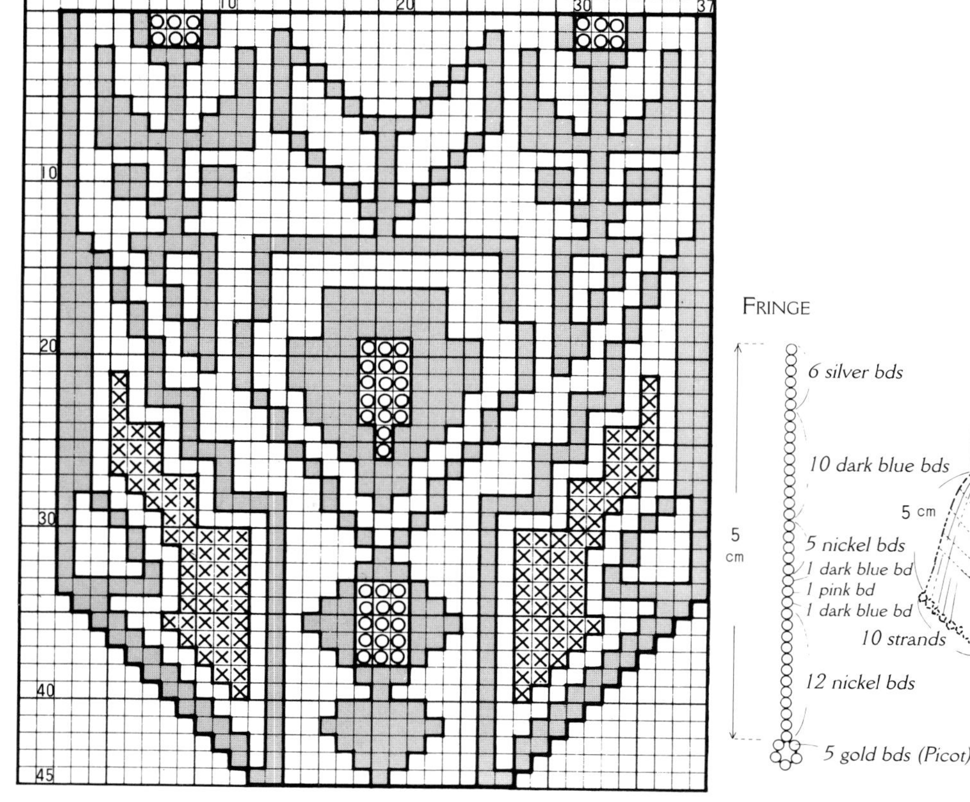

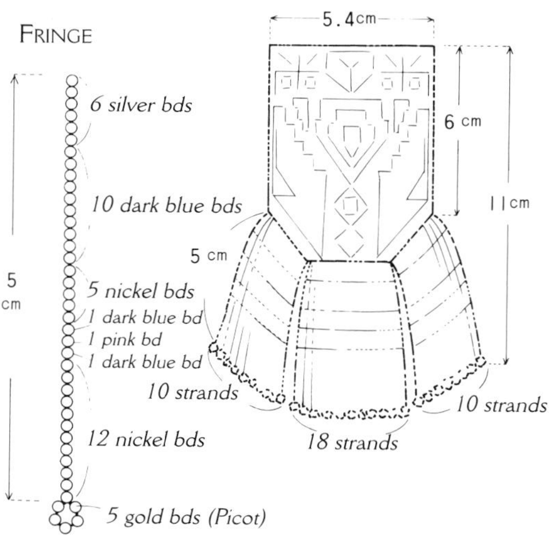

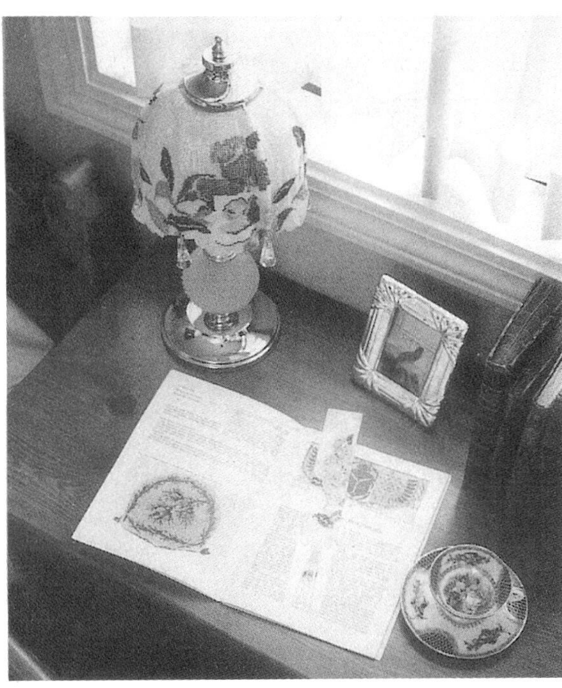

Peaceful Time

Pictured on page 44

Rose Bookmark

Finished size: 3.5cm x 22cm

● MATERIALS

Beads .... Listed on chart, pgage 124
Thread .... Beige
Supplies .... White Ribbon Tape, 3.5cm x 23cm
Horizontal & Vertical Rows .... 24 x 84

● PROCEDURE

Warp 25 threads, 60cm., Attach 5 fringes on the panel end and finish both ends. Stitch it with ribbon tape.

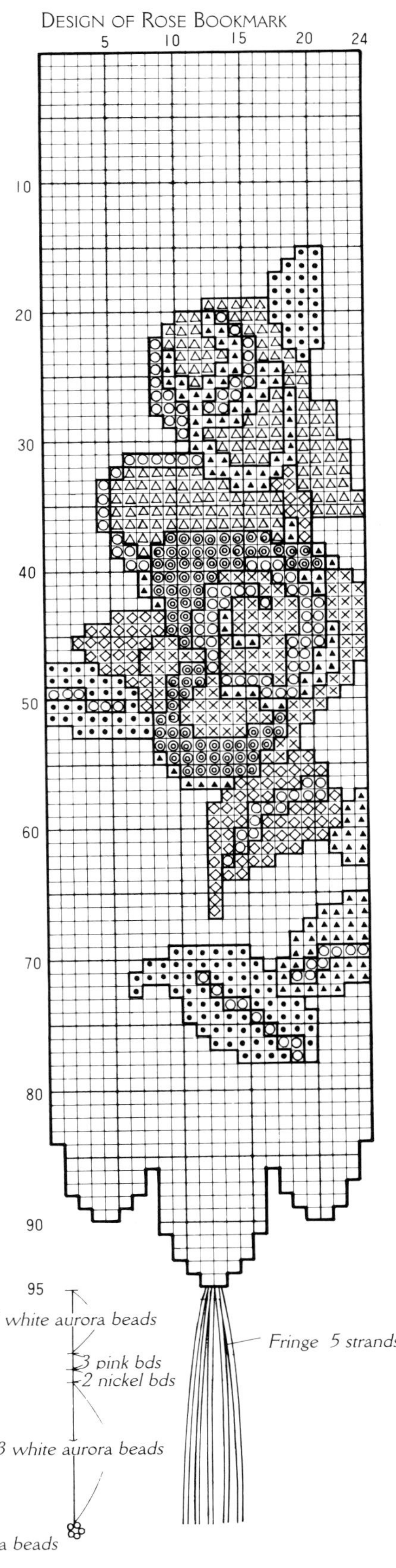

Stitch Chart for Rose Bookmark

□ = White Aurora (TB161) 10g
● = Charcoal Gray (TB81) 1g
△ = Pink (TB553) 2g
○ = Silver (TB558) 1g
▲ = Nickel (TB711) 1g
◇ = Yellow Green (TB775) 1g
× = Yellow (TB902) 1g
◎ = White Aurora (TB777) 1g

1	24												
∫	∫												
14	24												
15	19	2●	3										
16	18	3●	3										
17	17	4●	3										
18	17	4●	3										
19	12	5△	4●	3									
20	10	2△	1▲	1○	3△	4●	3						
21	9	3△	2▲	1○	3△	3●	3						
22	8	1○	4△	2▲	1○	2△	3●	3					
23	8	1○	1▲	4△	1▲	1○	3△	1●	4				
24	8	1○	1▲	3△	2▲	1○	2▲	2△	4				
25	8	1○	2▲	1△	2▲	2△	2▲	2△	4				
26	8	2○	3▲	2○	2▲	1△	1▲	1△	4				
27	8	3○	1▲	2○	2▲	2△	1▲	3△	2				
28	9	2○	4▲	3△	1▲	3△	2						
29	10	1○	1▲	6△	1▲	3△	2						
30	11	2▲	5△	1▲	4△	1							
31	6	6○	2▲	3△	2▲	4△	1						
32	5	1○	6△	6▲	1□	4△	1						
33	4	1○	9△	3▲	2□	4△	1						
34	4	1○	13△	2□	4△								
35	4	1○	13△	2□	4△								
36	4	1○	13△	1▲	1□	4							
37	5	1○	3△	8◎	1△	1▲	1□	4					
38	5	2○	1△	12◎	1▲	3							
39	6	2○	7◎	3○	3◎	1▲	2						
40	7	1▲	5◎	4×	2○	2▲	2×	1					
41	7	1▲	4◎	4○	2×	2○	1▲	3×					
42	8	1▲	3◎	2○	2×	1○	2×	2○	3×				
43	5	4□	2◎	2○	1▲	5×	2○	3×					
44	3	6□	2◎	2○	1▲	5×	2○	1▲	2×				
45	2	6□	2×	1◎	2○	1×	2▲	2×	3○	1▲	2×		
46	3	4□	5×	1○	5×	2	2▲	2×					
47	4●	3□	3×	2◎	1○	5×	2○	2▲	1×	1			
48	6●	2□	1×	3◎	1×	4○	1×	1○	2▲	2×	1		
49	3○	4●	1□	1×	2◎	2×	3▲	3○	1▲	2×	2		
50	3●	3○	1●	1□	1×	1◎	6×	2▲	3×	3			
51	8●	2◎	7×	1◎	2×	4							
52	2	6●	3◎	4×	3◎	1×	5						
53	8	9◎	2×	5									

54	8	1▲	7◎	2×	2□	4							
55	9	1▲	6◎	5□	3								
56	10	4▲	5□	2○	3								
57	13	4□	4○	1□	1	1▲							
58	12	3□	3○	4□	2▲								
59	12	3□	1○	6□	2▲								
60	12	2□	2○	5□	3▲								
61	12	2□	1○	4□	2	3▲							
62	12	1□	1○	3□	5	2▲							
63	12	3□	9										
64	12	1□	11										
65	12	1□	9	2▲									
66	12	1□	7	4▲									
67	19	5▲											
68	18	6▲											
69	9	6●	3	2▲	4○								
70	7	9●	1	2▲	2○	3▲							
71	6	5●	1○	5●	1▲	2○	4▲						
72	6	1●	2	3●	1○	4●	5▲	2					
73	10	3●	2○	4●	5								
74	10	5●	1○	4●	4								
75	11	5●	1○	3●	4								
76	12	5●	2○	1●	4								
77	14	4●	1○	1●	4								
78	24												
79	24												
80	24												
81	24												
82	24												
83	24												
84	①	22	①										
85	①	22	①										
86	①	6	①	8	①	6	①						
87	①	6	①	8	①	5	②						
88	②	4	②	8	②	4	②						
89	③	2	③	8	③	2	③						
90	⑧	8	⑧										
91	⑨	6	⑨										
92	⑨	6	⑨										
93	⑩	4	⑩										
94	⑪	2	⑪										

BEAD WEAVING TECHNIQUE

Weaving with beads is unlike basic weaving where the weft, or cross-wise threads go over and under the warp threads to create a structural fabric.

In bead weaving, there is a double weft thread, one thread going under all warp threads and the other going over all warp threads, both threads going through the single hole in each bead which falls between all warp threads. Refer to Page 53.

Weaving in this manner requires no shed, all warp threads remaining parallel. Spacing is controlled, not by any outside spacer but by the beads themselves.

Bead weaving is thus quite simple and much closer to the charted techniques of cross stitch and filet, where the main concern is deciding which bead is placed between each pair of warp threads as called for by the corresponding square of your chart.

In weaving narrow bands, the selected beads for each row are placed onto your weft thread and then pushed up from below with your finger, one bead falling between each pair of warp threads. The threaded weft thread is then passed around the outer warp thread(s) and returned to the opposite side, passing through each bead, but this time running on top of the warp threads. It is a good practice to wrap the weft thread one or two times around the outer warp thread prior to the return to secure each row. The beads are then threaded for the next row. The passing of the upper thread will always be in the same direction, typically right-to-left if right-handed.

In weaving wide patterned pieces, those over 4", this procedure is difficult and certainly time consuming as the many beads of each row need to be carefully counted and placed on the weft thread in the precise sequence required with no margin for error.

Many of the rich projects and patterns presented in this book will require the use of a wide beading loom, specifically designed for this purpose and the simple *two needle weaving technique* described below will make bead weaving a joy.

For wide pieces, a two needle method is suggested, using 2 separate weft threads. This will eliminate the pre-counting of beads and will permit the placement of one or more individual beads as the work proceeds. It permits beading as you go and is definitely more fun.

Referring to *FIG. 1*, a standard length blunt pointed beading needle is used on the lower weft thread to pick up the beads and a long blunt pointed beading needle is used on the upper weft thread to pass this thread through the beads as they are placed between the warp threads. Thus when doing a background of the same color, a large quantity of uncounted beads can be threaded and incorporated into the weaving. When you get near the design, excess beads can be dropped off and the selected color beads can be threaded in small manageable units. A blunt needle is necessary to avoid splitting the warp threads when passing though the beads. In passing the upper (long) needle, take care that one bead lies between each pair of warp threads. Referring to *FIG. 2*, at end warp threads, cross upper and lower weft threads.

As you will be most comfortable in passing the threaded weft in one direction, typically right-to-left if right-handed, it will be necessary to rotate the loom, 180° after the completion of each row. For comfort, the weaving area is best kept in the middle of the loom.

In working with many colors of beads the following techniques should be noted.

For background and large areas of one color, it is suggested that you work from strung beads which are typically sold in hanks with strands approximately 18" long. Beads are easily transferred from the strung put-up to your beading needle thread by simply running the needle through the beads while keeping the strand taut.

For the areas of design requiring many color changes, it is suggested that you lay lengths of double sticky tape on an index card or other stiff material and dump a small quantity of beads onto the card. Selected beads are easily picked up from this card with your threaded short needle.

Two Needle Bead Weaving Technique

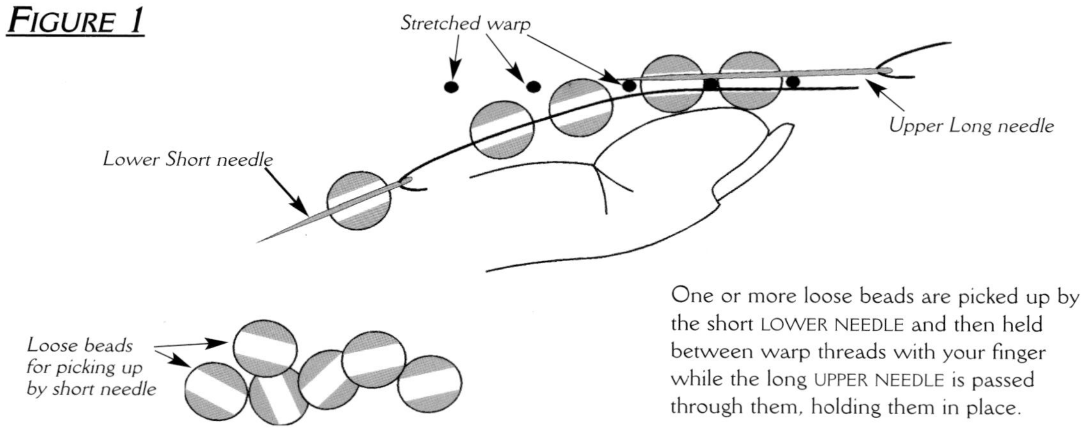

One or more loose beads are picked up by the short LOWER NEEDLE and then held between warp threads with your finger while the long UPPER NEEDLE is passed through them, holding them in place.

The LACIS bead loom, illustrated in *Fig 3,* is specifically designed for 2-needle wide bead weaving. Set up and warping is done in a matter of minutes and the loom is designed to be used from either end. It incorporates integral warp tension control and when used with its related floor stand, illustrated in *Fig 4,* it is easily rotated after the completion of each row. The active weaving area is maintained in the center of the loom by simple warp rotation as the work proceeds.

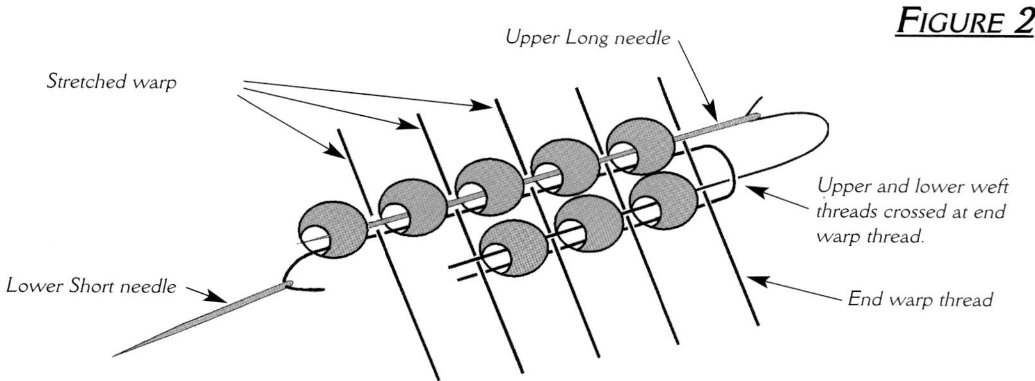

SHORT NEEDLE and thread always remains under warp threads while LONG NEEDLE always remains over warp threads. Cross or wrap threads around end warp thread.

Symmetrical design permits weaving from either side as required for 2-needle weaving.
Eccentrically mounted end frame bars permit simple tension control and warp rotation.
Continuous warp is quickly prepared and permits rotation around frame as weaving progresses
Board resting on lower warp threads supports design cartoon.
Strand of beads of same size as being woven serves as warp spacer.
Legs raise frame for ease of working and serve as warping frame for extended warps.
Bead loom
Quick release for removal of loom
Incline adjustment and lock
Rotating yoke permits weaving from both sides of loom as required for 2-needle weaving.
Adjustable for sit-down or stand-up weaving with full height adjustment.
Stand assembles and disassembles without tools and fits compactly into a 18" x 6' x 6" space.

LACIS BEAD LOOM

FIGURE 3

FIGURE 4

BEAD LOOM MOUNTED ON FLOOR STAND

Some basic materials and accessories recommended for bead weaving are:

Thread: Bonded nylon is recommended. It is very strong 3-ply tight twisted thread which will not untwist and is resistant to splitting. Size "B" or "C" is suggested , depending on the size of the bead. "B" for size 11 and finer and "C" for larger beads.

Magnet: A basic accessory which, when attached to the side of the loom, will keep the needles in place and out of the way when not being used.

Holder Clip: A device which attaches to the loom for holding your pattern above the working area.

Bead Organizer: A compartmented container to keep the various color beads separated.

Bead Weaving Grid: A transparent grid in the proportion of a full size #11 seed bead. Any design can be accurately translated to a woven bead pattern by laying the grid over the design to be copied and simply following the predominate color in each square.

LACIS PUBLISHES AND DISTRIBUTES BOOKS SPECIFICALLY RELATED TO THE TEXTILE ARTS, FOCUSING ON THE SUBJECTS OF LACE AND LACE MAKING, COSTUME, EMBROIDERY AND HAND SEWING.

OTHER LACIS BOOKS OF INTEREST:

THE CARE AND PRESERVATION OF TEXTILES, KAREN FINCH & GRETA PUTNAM
THE ART OF HAIR WORK, MARK CAMPBELL
CROSS-STITCH ALPHABETS & TREASURES, ED. BY JULES & KAETHE KLIOT
SMOCKING & FINE SEWING, ED BY JULES & KAETHE KLIOT
MODERN DANCING (1914), MR & MRS VERNON CASTLE
MILLINERY FOR EVERY WOMAN, GEORGINA KERR KAYE
TECHNIQUE OF LADIES' HAIR DRESSING (19TH C.): CAMPBELL & MALLEMONT
KNITTING: 19TH C. SOURCES: ED. JULES & KAETHE KLIOT
HAUTE COUTURE EMBROIDERY: THE ART OF LESAGE, PALMER WHITE
THE MARY FRANCES SEWING BOOK, JANE EAYRE FRYER
THE MARY FRANCES KNITTING AND CROCHETING BOOK, JANE EAYRE FRYER
THE MARY FRANCES HOUSEKEEPER, JANE EAYRE FRYER
THE MARY FRANCES COOK BOOK, JANE EAYRE FRYER
THE MARY FRANCES GARDEN BOOK, JANE EAYRE FRYER
NETTING: FROM EARLY SOURCES, ED. JULES & KAETHE KLIOT
CROCHET: EDGINGS & INSERTIONS, ELIZA A. TAYLOR & BELLE ROBINSON
CROCHET: EDGINGS & MORE, ED. JULES & KAETHE KLIOT
CROCHET: NOVELTIES, ED. JULES & KAETHE KLIOT
CROCHET: MORE EDGINGS, ED. JULES & KAETHE KLIOT
CROCHET: DOLLS & NOVELTIES, ED. JULES & KAETHE KLIOT
THE NEEDLE MADE LACES OF RETICELLA. ED JULES & KAETHE KLIOT
CASALGUIDI STYLE LINEN EMBROIDERY, EFFIE MITROFANIS
THE ART OF SHETLAND LACE, SARAH DON
CREATING ORIGINAL HAND-KNITTED LACE, MARGARET STOVE
BERLIN WORK, SAMPLERS & EMBROIDERY OF THE 19TH C. RAFFAELLA SERENA
THE MAGIC OF FREE MACHINE EMBROIDERY, DOREEN CURRAN
DESIGNS FOR CHURCH EMBROIDERIES, THOMAS BROWN & SON
EMBROIDERY WITH BEADS, ANGELA THOMPSON
BEADED BAGS AND MORE, ED. BY JULES & KAETHE KLIOT
BEAD EMBROIDERY, JOAN EDWARDS
BEAD EMBROIDERY, VALERIE CAMPBELL-HARDING AND PAMELA WATTS
INNOVATIVE BEADED JEWELRY TECHNIQUES, GINEKE ROOT
BEADED ANIMALS IN JEWELRY, LETTY LAMMENS AND ELS SCHOLTE
CLASSIC BEADED PURSE PATTERNS, E. DE JONG-KRAMER
BEAD WEAVING: ACCESSORIES, TAKAKO SAKO
LOCKER HOOKING, LEONE PEGUERO
TATTED LACE OF BEADS: TECHNIQUE OF BEANILE LACE, NINA LIBIN
TATTING: DESIGNS FROM VICTORIAN LACE CRAFT, ED.BY JULES & KAETHE KLIOT
THE ART OF TATTING, KATHERINE HOARE
TATTING WITH VISUAL PATTERNS, MARY KONIOR
PRACTICAL TATTING, PHYLLIS SPARKS
NEW DIMENSIONS IN TATTING, TO DE HAAN-VAN BEEK
THE DMC BOOK OF CHARTED TATTING DESIGNS, KIRSTINE & INGE NIKOLAJSEN
THE ART OF NETTING, JULES & KAETHE KLIOT
TENERIFFE LACE, JULES & KAETHE KLIOT
THE BARGELLO BOOK, FRANCES SALTER
FLORENTINE EMBROIDERY, BARBARA MULLER

FOR A COMPLETE LIST OF LACIS TITLES, WRITE TO:

LACIS
3163 ADELINE STREET
BERKELEY, CA 94703 USA